The Meaning of Anglican Catholicism

By Fr Jonathan Munn OblOSB

Published by the Anglican Catholic Church – Diocese of the United Kingdom
https://www.anglicancatholic.org.uk/

© 2021 Fr Jonathan Munn OblOSB. All rights reserved.
ISBN 978-1-008-92799-5

PREFACE

There are a lot of enquiries about the Anglican Catholic Church: many are very genuine in their intent to understand what it is about this Church that makes it unique; others enquire in order to decry or denounce the Church as not being genuine. These latter are folk who equate "Anglican Catholicism" with "Anglo-Catholicism" and "Affirming Catholicism" and who insist that they (usually members of the Anglican Communion) are true Anglican Catholics in opposition to the Anglican Catholic Church. This is not altogether unsurprising: to many, the words "Anglican" and "Catholic" have had their meanings altered to "include" people who would otherwise be excluded on account of their own personal beliefs. If we say the Nicene Creed and claim that we believe in "One, Holy, Catholic and Apostolic Church" but hold to different meanings of "One", "Holy", "Catholic" and "Apostolic" then how can we be committing ourselves to the same belief – the same Faith! – as the countless Christians who have held them dear and even shed their blood when those words were finally ratified at the Council of Constantinople in AD381?

This essay seeks to address this ambiguity by demonstrating that not only that the Anglican Catholic Church is well-named but also that it is utterly consistent with the understanding of those who were present at the origin of the terms "Anglican" and "Catholic". The bulk of this essay forms the author's thesis accepted by the Johann Heinrich Pestalozzi Christian University for the degree of MTh and intends to show what Anglican Catholicism means as opposed to what people want it to mean.

CONTENTS

ACKNOWLEDGEMENTS VII

INTRODUCTION 8

Evolution of Language 8

Sources, References and Abbreviations 10

CYRILLIC-VINCENTIAN CATHOLICISM AND THE ACC 11

Principles of Authority 11

    The Historical Record and Holy Scripture 11

    A Note on Miracles 14

    The Christianity of the Old Testament 19

    The Place of Tradition 20

    The Patristic Use of Reason 22

According to the Whole 24

    St Ignatius of Antioch 24

    St Cyril of Jerusalem 25

    St Vincent and his Canon 27

    The Reflexivity of the Vincentian Canon 29

A Note on Reason 32

    Dianoia   32

        A More Positive View 34

A Note on Experience 36

    Spong and Schori 36

    Apostolic Experience 38

- Experience in the Theological Science 40
- The Necessity of Experience 42
- The Holy Ghost and the Unity of the Faith 43

Anglican Catholicism and Cyrillic-Vincentian Catholicism 47
- Holy Scriptures 49
- The Creeds 51
- Tradition 59

Conclusion 60

IGNATIAN CATHOLICISM AND THE ACC 62

Orthokoinōnia 64
- The meaning of Communion 64
- The Communion of the Saints 66

The Body and Blood of Christ 69
- The Real Presence 70
- The Sacrifice of the Mass 72
- The Necessity of the Priesthood 76

The Priesthood 79
- The Priesthood Intended 79
- Levi and Melchisedek 80
- Function and Character 82
- The Apostolic Succession 85

Anglican Catholicism and Ignatian Catholicism 87
- Eucharistic Theology as the Locus of Communion 87
- The Internal View of the Anglican Catholic Priesthood 91

    The ACC and Orthodox Orders 92

    Apostolicae Curae and the ACC 93

Conclusion 98

ANGLICANISM AND THE ACC 100

The Question of Anglican Identity 101

    Anglicanism and Wittgenstein 104

    The Anglican Succession of the ACC 108

    Anglicanism ad fontem 112

    The Book of Common Prayer 113

Protestantism and Anglicanism 117

    The Meaning of being Protestant 119

    How is Anglicanism Protestant? 121

    The Protestant Book of Common Prayer? 125

    The Thirty-Nine Articles 131

    The Catalyst for the Congress 133

    What does the ACC continue? 135

Conclusion 140

CONCLUSIONS AND FURTHER DIRECTIONS 142

    The Principle of Theologoumena 142

    Modernism 144

    Unity   145

    Struggle   145

    Final words 146

DEDICATION

To the most Holy and Undivided Trinity, to the crucified humanity of Our Lord Jesus Christ, to the fruitful virginity of the blessed and most glorious Virgin Mary, to Holy Benedict, father of monks and St Thomas Aquinas and all the saints be everlasting praise, honour, power and glory throughout all ages, world without end.

ACKNOWLEDGEMENTS

Thanks must go to Bishop Damien Mead and the Venerable Raymond Thompson for their much appreciated inspiration, preaching, and direction, and for inviting me into a spiritual home where I have thrived for the past decade. Thanks also to Fr Andrew Scurr for his invaluable thoughts and willingness to hear my ideas and for asking awkward questions (upon my invitation!).

Thanks also to Professors Stewart Thompson, Craig Paterson and Canon Peter Thompson, and indeed to the Johann Heinrich Pestalozzi University for their exemplary encouragement and scholarly advice which have allowed me to organize my thoughts and bring me back into the academic milieu which I have sorely missed, and whose stimulating questions have allowed me to develop some of my ideas beyond my initial thinking.

Finally, thanks to my wife and children who have always loved me, stood by me, supported me and nursed my shins following multiple barkings on the baby-gate.

Introduction

Evolution of Language

Words change their meaning. While this is a healthy phenomenon by which mankind finds ways of communicating new ideas to contemporaries about contemporary issues, it produces difficulties for those who seek to engage in dialogue with those in the past. In the past thirty years, "wicked!" has come to mean "great!", and "sick!" has come to mean "beautiful!": yet even these words are now regarded as *passé* among the young people of the current age. In order to understand the past, even from a few decades ago, there has to be a translation of the language of the past into the language of the present.

This evolution of language is most problematic when Christians seek to understand "Jesus Christ the same yesterday, and to day, and for ever."[1] There is only one Lord Jesus Christ and He is the eternal Truth. The Gospels record His single Incarnation, His one, perfect oblation for us upon the cross and His glorious resurrection from the dead: these are eternal truths about Him for they are facts about God albeit in time. These events have indeed occurred at one point in our time but the resulting Gospel applies to all humanity throughout time.

The way that language changes affects how the Gospel is to be understood. Our Lord says, "when ye fast..."[2]: is He presenting a hypothetical situation about fasting that many might assume today, or is He presenting an expectation of His followers to fast at a time in which fasting is more commonplace and extending that expectation to the present day? If language evolves to the extent that "wicked!" can mean "good!" then it is possible that the present understanding of "resurrection" today might not necessarily be the same understanding of "resurrection" when the stone was rolled away from the mouth of the tomb. If language evolves and meanings of words change, how can the Church today be sure that Gospel it preaches is the Gospel which God bids it preach? This evolution makes it especially difficult when St Paul's words to the Galatians are considered:

---

[1] Hebrews xiii.8
[2] St Matthew vi.16

> As we said before, so say I now again, If any man preach any
> other gospel unto you than that ye have received, let him be
> accursed.[3]

If the gospel that the Church preaches is no longer the Gospel it once preached, then how can it be the Gospel? What fate awaits a church with a gospel that has altered?

In being the same yesterday, today and forever, the truths Our Lord speaks are truths for all of us independent of our age and culture. The Divine Eternity – i.e. the timelessness of God – gives temporal beings the challenge to understand divine revelation and communicate it through the centuries.

It is on account of the evolution of language that the schism of East and West gradually unfurled and Christians began to talk past each other with greater consequences to the Church than those of the previous centuries, most notably the confusion between Miaphysitism and Monophysitism following the Council of Chalcedon in AD451.

Today, the same problem in language is faced once more as ideas are being tested within Christianity and the message is being altered or even lost. The Anglican Catholic Church (ACC) arose out of the storm within The Episcopal Church of the United States of America (ECUSA) at a time when the doctrine of the priesthood was being redefined and the language of prayer changed. One of the results of the separation from ECUSA has been the need for the ACC to justify itself to all enquirers, some who have been distinctly hostile. Objections have been raised: can one be truly Anglican if one is not in communion with the Archbishop of Canterbury? Can one be truly Catholic if one is Anglican? Can one be truly Anglican if one is Catholic?

The purpose of this essay is to make some headway in demonstrating that the Anglican Catholic Church is well-named by showing that it is truly Catholic and therefore Orthodox; by showing that it is truly Anglican despite the vagueness of that term; and by showing how it is a Continuing Anglican Church in its continuation of a significant thread of self-understanding which originated in the Church of England, as exemplified in the Oxford Movement, and which was discontinued in the Church of England and ECUSA over the course of the latter half of the twentieth century in their changes to doctrine.

---

[3] Galatians i.9

The method will be to return to *ad fontes verborum* as far as possible and chart how words were used in the formative period of the Primitive Church, and show that the ACC fulfils the definitions and criteria as those recognised by the Church when those definitions and criteria were made and so is as it claims to be. The reasonability of the Catholic principles of authority, namely Holy Scripture, Tradition and Right Reason, is demonstrated and thus used to show that the ACC has the same basis of authority as the Roman Catholic and Orthodox Churches. Although the word "Anglican" has a variety of meanings – not wholly consistent – it will be shown that there is a sense in which it can be given a Catholic meaning and that this is precisely how Anglican Catholicism understands itself.

Sources, References and Abbreviations

In this work, the Authorised Version will be used as the standard translation of the Bible since this is the version canonically regulated by the ACC. The only exception to this will be that the Psalms will be quoted as they appear in the modern spelling of the 1662 Book of Common Prayer. Many of the quotations from the Church Fathers may be found in the three volume series compiled by Schaff, Donaldson and others. The abbreviation ANF will be used when referring to the Ante-Nicene Fathers (Donaldson, et al., 1994 (Reprinted 2012)), NPNF1 when referring to the first series of Nicene and Post-Nicene Fathers (Schaff, 2004) and NPNF2 when referring to second series (Schaff, et al., 1996).

Further, the thematic indices from Jurgens' work Faith of the Early Fathers (Jurgens, 1970) will be used under the abbreviation FEF together with the paragraph numbers found therein. Some parts of this essay will be restatements from the author's previous publications such as (Munn, 2019) and his weblog which may be found at http://warwickensis.blogspot.com.

Cyrillic-Vincentian Catholicism and the ACC

Principles of Authority

It is necessary to begin, then, with what Anglican Catholicism understands by authoritative revelation – how does the Church decide what is truly what God has told her and is telling her? The Christian must begin with the person of Jesus Christ.

The Historical Record and Holy Scripture

There is much disagreement among scholars about who Jesus was. Some, like Dr Bart Ehrman (Ehrman, 2015), do not believe that Jesus taught that He was the Son of God and that biblical texts have been altered for the purpose of divinising Him.[4] Ehrman's bias is that he cannot believe that miracles happen, i.e. water cannot spontaneously become wine, nor can the dead be raised. For him, if the historical record says that a miracle happened, then the historical record must have been tampered with.[5] Thus, for Ehrman, miracles can never have a record in history even if they did actually happen. It can be seen from this that the opinions and beliefs of historians do colour radically their interpretation of historical sources.

Here, then, is the historical fact of the person of Jesus of Nazareth called the Christ by His followers.[6] The Church has therefore collated as much information about Him as it can find. As a result of this collation, there are the four Gospels which, though denounced by scholars such as Ehrman, Funk[7] and Bultmann as unreliable, nonetheless demonstrate greater reliability once one becomes less fixated upon the unscientific premise that "miracles cannot happen". As Peter J. Williams says:

---

[4] See (Komoszewski, et al., 2006) p 103ff, (Williams, 2018) p 111ff
[5] (Ehrman, 2009) p 146-147 and throughout.
[6] Even Ehrman does not doubt the existence of Jesus of Nazareth. (Ehrman, 2012)
[7] Robert Funk, founder of the Jesus Seminar which, among other findings declared that Jesus was not born in Bethlehem, did not walk on water, used ancient medicine to cure psychosomatic diseases and, most importantly, declared the Jesus did not rise from the dead. See Funk, The Acts of Jesus: The Search for the Authentic Deeds, 1998, San Francisco, Harper

> ... it is rational to have a high degree of confidence in the text of the Gospels as it appears in modern editions. These editions themselves indicate where uncertainties lie.[8]

Williams, like many other scholars,[9] spends a great deal of time showing that the history recorded within the Gospels is indeed true and that the Gospels provide eye-witness statements. If the Gospels are true then this Jesus of Nazareth can be none other than the Son of Man, Son of God, the Logos and thus God Himself to whom the Christian should refer with the deepest respect as Our Lord. Again, with other scholars, Williams favours an early dating of the Gospels and even those who favour a later dating will put the four canonical Gospels within a century of the events they record. Saints Clement of Rome (AD35-AD99)[10], Ignatius of Antioch (d AD108)[11] and Polycarp of Smyrna (AD 69 -AD155) are said to have known the apostles[12] and their teaching and their testimony would thus be available to correct any defect in the Gospels. Hence, unfortunately for Ehrman, the Gospels were written in living memory of eye-witnesses to Jesus' life and death and could easily be proved (or disproved) simply by asking one of these witnesses.[13]

Any search for this real Jesus and the realisation of His achievement for Mankind must take into account these eye-witness statements about Him and how His Church develops through the influence of the Holy Ghost that His Father sends. The eye-witness accounts can, and do, scandalise modern ears and view of science with talk of miracle, angel and resurrection.[14] Perhaps this forms the beginning of the challenge that Christians face in this modern age: the Gospel is a challenge in every time and every place and there will be resistance to it from the secular element. If a gospel becomes acceptable to a culture, then that cannot be the true Gospel because

---

[8] (Williams, 2018) p 122

[9] Such as (Wallace (ed), 2011), (Evans, 2007) and (Craig, 2010) to name a few.

[10] Possibly the Clement mentioned in Philippians iv.3 but most likely to be the Clement mentioned in The Shepherd of Hermas, Vision Second.iv.3, (ANF II p 12). His first letter is considered to be one of the earliest outside of the Biblical canon. (Carrier, Richard (2014). On the Historicity of Jesus, Sheffield. Phoenix Press. p 271–272)

[11] The traditional date given by Eusebius. Timothy Barnes (The Expository Times, 120 (3): 119–130) suggests that Ignatius quotes the Gnostic Ptolemy who is active at AD130 and thus dates the death of Ignatius at AD140.

[12] St Irenaeus states that St Polycarp and St Papias heard St John preach in *Adversus Haereses* V.xxxiii.4 (ANF I p563).

[13] See (Williams, 2018) p 48. The table shows clearly that even the latest dating of St John's Gospel by Ehrman is AD95 which is 62 years after the traditional date of the Crucifixion. St Mark's is dated to about AD65 which is 32 years – well within living memory, indeed close to the traditional dates of the deaths of St Peter and St Paul.

[14] As the vast quantity of material by atheists over the centuries shows, not least the famous diatribe by Richard Dawkins. (Dawkins, 2006) p 31

the first word that Our Lord says in His adult ministry is, "Repent!"[15] If an age has no need of repentance then Heaven on Earth has been achieved through the efforts of Man because all have turned to Christ through their will. This rather contradicts the vision of St John the Divine:

> And I saw a new heaven and a new earth: for the first heaven and the first earth were passed away; and there was no more sea. And I John saw the holy city, new Jerusalem, coming down from God out of heaven, prepared as a bride adorned for her husband. And I heard a great voice out of heaven saying, Behold, the tabernacle of God is with men, and he will dwell with them, and they shall be his people, and God himself shall be with them, and be their God. And God shall wipe away all tears from their eyes; and there shall be no more death, neither sorrow, nor crying, neither shall there be any more pain: for the former things are passed away. And he that sat upon the throne said, Behold, I make all things new.[16]

If there is no need of repentance then the New Heaven and the New Earth have not come down out of Heaven but rather any newness has come from Man not from God contradicting what is revealed here.

One further point must be made and this is to do with one of Ehrman's assumptions that there is no single Christianity but rather a selection of Christianities from which the Orthodox Doctrine emerged as a victor from a series of political battles. This is a misrepresentation by Walter Bauer of the facts of the unanimity of Christian doctrine as revealed by the very existence of Holy Scripture itself, though Bauer and Ehrman tend to read Scripture in the light of their acceptance of the multi-doctrinal hypothesis. This is the basis for a pluralism which modern theologians read into the Early Church and which is patently false as Andreas Köstenberger and Michael Kruger demonstrate:

> The Bauer-Ehrman thesis is invalid. Earliest Christianity was not infested with a plethora of competing heresies (or "Christianities," as Ehrman and other Bauer paragons prefer to call them); it was a largely unified movement that had coalesced around the conviction that Jesus was the Messiah and exalted Lord predicted in the Old Testament. Consequently, the apostles preached Jesus crucified, buried, and risen on the third day according to the Scriptures. There were heretics, for sure, but the trajectory spanning from the

---

[15] St Matthew iv.17
[16] Revelation xxi.1-5

> Old Testament to Jesus and the apostles provided a clear and compelling infrastructure and mechanism by which the earliest Christians could judge whether a given teaching conformed to its doctrinal christological core or deviated from it.[17]

There is only One Faith and that is clear from the Scriptures and Apostolic Fathers.

A Note on Miracles

As stated above, much modern scholarship rejects the miraculous nature of the New Testament. Rudolf Bultmann is notable for regarding the historicity of the New Testament as a waste of time:

Contemporary Christian proclamation is faced with the question whether, when it demands faith from men and women, it expects them to acknowledge this mythical world picture from the past. If this is impossible, it has to face the question whether the New Testament proclamation has a truth that is independent of the mythical world picture, in which case it would be the task of theology to demythologize the Christian proclamation.[18]

As has already been seen, historians of the same mindset as Ehrman follow Bultmann's programme of "demythologization" one step further in order to argue for the unreliability of the New Testament accounts based on the presumption that miracles cannot happen. The more famous arguments against miracles come from David Hume. Essentially, Hume summarises his maxim:

> "That no testimony is sufficient to establish a miracle, unless the testimony be of such a kind, that its falsehood would be more miraculous, than the fact, which it endeavours to establish; and even in that case there is a mutual destruction of arguments, and the superior only gives us an assurance suitable to that degree of force, which remains, after deducting the inferior."[19]

William Lane Craig and J. P Moreland make one refutation of Hume's arguments using the fact that Hume does not understand mathematical probability theory.[20]

---

[17] (Kostenberger, et al., 2010) p233
[18] Rudolf Bultmann, *Neues Testament und Mythologie* (1941), as translated by Schubert M. Ogden (1984)
[19] David Hume, An Essay Concerning Human Understanding, Section X.91
[20] (Craig, et al., 2003) p 569-570

The scientific method states that the stronger the evidence, the more likely the truth of the hypothesis.

For example, in the COVID 19 pandemic, a test for the virus needs to be accurate and this means reducing the probability of false positives. The probability that needs to be calculated is, "given that a person does not have the virus, how likely is it that the test is positive?" The same is true for miracles: the evidence for the truth of a miracle is its test and thus it is necessary to ask the question, "given that the miracle is false how likely is it that that evidence shows that it is true?" Applying this to the statements of five hundred people who witness Our Lord alive after His crucifixion and the likelihood of the truth of the Resurrection becomes a lot higher than Hume might allow.

Nor does Hume consider that probability is not the same as possibility. The odds of winning the lottery are roughly fourteen million to one, and yet one set of numbers will come up despite there being a tiny probability of that particular set that does occur. Further, the theory of quantum tunnelling suggests that it is entirely possible that, while he lived, every atom in Hume's body might have spontaneously appeared on Mars for a couple of seconds before returning to their more usual location. The probability is astronomically minute and it would take a period of time longer than the lifetime of the observable universe for it to happen just once: it still remains a possibility within the understanding of modern science. It is not logically impossible to imagine that a dead man might live again, nor is it logically impossible to imagine a multitude being fed on five loaves of bread. They are highly unlikely occurrences and yet, should they occur, according to Hume, they would break logic itself.

Hume's disproof of miracles from miracles[21] says that,

1) If miracles are true then the religion to which they belong is true.

2) Miracles happen in every religion.

3) Therefore all religions are true.

4) But religions contradict each other.

5) Thus miracles cannot happen.

One major flaw, however, in Hume's argument is that he defines the term "miracle" rather than rely on how miracles are seen within religious cultures. His definition is:

---

[21] David Hume, An Essay Concerning Human Understanding, Section X.95

> A miracle is a violation of the laws of nature; and as a firm and unalterable experience has established these laws, the proof against a miracle, from the very nature of the fact, is as entire as any argument from experience can possibly be imagined.[22]

Is this the understanding of miracles that the Catholic Church possesses? If not, then it would seem reasonable to assume that Hume is making a colossal straw man argument.

First, the word "miracle" itself is derived from the Latin *miro* meaning wonderful. The word admiration comes from the Latin *admiror* which means to marvel at. In this definition, there is nothing about violating the Laws of Nature but rather refers to an event that makes the viewer sit up and take notice. The word "miracle" is used to translate the Greek words δύναμις[23] (a mighty work, power or virtue – a show of strength) and σημεῖον[24] (a sign or token). Unlikely though the Lord's works of power may be, it is His use of them to reinforce His teaching about the Kingdom of Heaven that matters not their explanation. Their point is not to stultify scientists in the twenty-first century but be recorded as signs and works of power that back up the teaching of the Lord. St Augustine takes a similar view:

Nevertheless, when we declare the miracles which God has wrought, or will yet work, and which we cannot bring under the very eyes of men, sceptics keep demanding that we shall explain these marvels to reason. And because we cannot do so, inasmuch as they are above human comprehension, they suppose we are speaking falsely. These persons themselves, therefore, ought to account for all these marvels which we either can or do see. And if they perceive that this is impossible for man to do, they should acknowledge that it cannot be concluded that a thing has not been or shall not be because it cannot be reconciled to reason, since there are things now in existence of which the same is true.[25]

To say that something is a miracle because it cannot be explained by Science risks an appeal to the "God of the Gaps" and this provides somewhat of a red herring to the nature of miracles. The time-reversibility[26] of Newton's Laws of Motion implies that it is perfectly possible to stir raw scrambled egg in such a way that it returns to the state in which it was when it was cracked into the bowl. None of the Lord's miracles is likely to be completely inexplicable by physics – though it is clear they

---

[22] David Hume, An Essay Concerning Human Understanding, Section X.90
[23] E.g. St Mark ix.39
[24] E.g. Exodus vii.9 (LXX), St Luke xxiii.8, St John iv.54
[25] St Augustine of Hippo, City of God XXI.v (NPNF1, II, p 455)
[26] That is, we may replace t by -t in the Newtonian Model and the equations of motion remain the same.

are far from simple conjuring tricks, especially the Resurrection – but there is a lack of a scientific record as to how they happened. It is worth noting that all of the Lord's miracles are consistent with natural processes. A dead man returns to life but a statue does not gain life; five loaves feed five thousand people but the bread does not become beef, nor stones bread; water becomes wine but a stone jar does not become a wedding cake.

And yet, according to Hume, if a brick were to be discovered actually floating in the air by an unsuspecting person there is no evidence that that individual could give to convince Hume of the truth. This rather renders Hume's metaphysics somewhat deficient as a means of discovering anything objectively true about the world: Hume cannot approve even of the Scientific Method. Writing in 1819, the Archbishop of Dublin, Richard Whately, used Hume's method to disprove the existence of Napoleon Bonaparte who was still alive and very much within living memory.[27] The Lord Himself is scathing of those who will only believe if they see the miracles they want to see:

Then certain of the scribes and of the Pharisees answered, saying, Master, we would see a sign from thee. But he answered and said unto them, An evil and adulterous generation seeketh after a sign; and there shall no sign be given to it, but the sign of the prophet Jonas: For as Jonas was three days and three nights in the whale's belly; so shall the Son of man be three days and three nights in the heart of the earth. The men of Nineveh shall rise in judgment with this generation, and shall condemn it: because they repented at the preaching of Jonas; and, behold, a greater than Jonas is here.[28]

From this it is clear that the Lord's miracles have a specific purpose for teaching His followers the truth: they are not a means of convincing people of who He is, though they may ease a growing conviction. There will be many miracles, even outside the Christian religion, but they need not necessarily be direct acts of God. The Devil can work wonders too as Job finds out.[29]

The Gospels cannot but be seen as eye-witness testimony, nor can the enquirer disregard the growth of the Church in the face of fierce, mortal persecution as the product of a philosophical misdirection, even if we might disbelieve the value of the

---

[27] Richard Whately, Historic Doubts Relative to Napoleon Buonaparte, Andover: Warren F. Draper, 1874.
[28] St Matthew xii.38-41
[29] E.g. Job i.2

testimony. Craig,[30] Evans[31] and Wallace[32] would certainly see Hume's attempt to disrupt the historical record as flawed. Indeed, Keith Ward says:

Hume is probably the greatest of those philosophers who reject the mainstream tradition with regard to God. But part of his greatness, in my view, lies precisely in the clarity and enormity of his mistakes, and in the way that they point to a philosophy that takes reason much more seriously.[33]

A miracle may have its explanation but it is the effect of its occurrence on the lives of those who witness it that matters. Clearly, something happened that altered unlearned fishermen to testify about Jesus Christ and go to their horrific deaths for that testimony. For miracles to be impossible, the human spirit must be incapable of wonder – perhaps the Humean spirit is. A Materialist worldview will indeed be enough to disregard all miracles but, if there is good evidence for the existence of God as demonstrated by the philosopher theologians then there is good evidence for the occurrence of miracles as occurrences beyond the understanding of human experience.

The moment that miracles become plausible, the more reasonable it is to take the Gospels at face-value. The testimony of the Gospel miracles is there for all to see but it will always be rejected by those whose hearts are hardened to the work of the Holy Ghost. Indeed, if God exists then miracles actually become not just plausible but necessary for the Christian Faith for the Resurrection can only be a miracle. By what scientific process does life return to a crucified corpse that has received a gaping cardiothoracic trauma? Further, how can a man who has received this trauma appear to eye-witnesses still bearing that very trauma to the extent that an observer can insert their hand into it? This certainly goes beyond medical science! If we see the miracle as an act that originates externally to Creation then no human science can be used to examine it. Scientific Materialism rejects miracles based on the assumption that Scientific Materialism is true. Yet, how can Scientific Materialism prove its assumption, or at least make it plausible? Where is the evidence that scientific evidence determines the truth? There needs to be a philosophical framework that determines the competence of Science to determine the truth and not the other way around. The existence of God and the miracles He performs are an immovable part of the Christian Faith whether Spong and Bultmann like it or not.

---

[30] (Craig, 2010)
[31] (Evans, 2007)
[32] (Wallace (ed), 2011)
[33] (Ward, 2009) p 75

The Christianity of the Old Testament

From the Gospels as central to the faith of the Church, the authority of Scripture may be seen to radiate back in time into the Old Testament. Our Lord Himself reminds us that if we forget about the Hebrew Bible then we miss the testimony about Him from those who have come before Him. As He walks with those on the road to Emmaus after His crucifixion, He upbraids them for their lack of theological perspicacity.

> O fools, and slow of heart to believe all that the prophets have spoken: Ought not Christ to have suffered these things, and to enter into his glory? And beginning at Moses and all the prophets, he expounded unto them in all the scriptures the things concerning himself.[34]

The Old Testament is a fundamental part of the Church's understanding of Christ, however, while it possesses its clear inspired testimony of God, it points outside itself towards a Messiah that is to come and is therefore necessarily incomplete until that Messiah comes. As the promised Messiah, Our Lord provides the lens[35] through which the Hebrew Bible must be read and thus become for Christians what is known as the Old Testament and, through the rapid consensus of the Church, as what constitutes authoritative Scripture. The famous Muratorian Fragment[36] demonstrates clearly that what is now known as the New Testament was nearly in place by the beginning of the Third Century. Further the Biblical canon is first shown to be complete in a synod in Rome,[37] a council in Hippo[38] and two councils of Carthage.[39] These councils did nothing other than restrict the reading in church of books other than those in the canon indicating that the Church was already well aware of the universal importance of these Holy Scriptures. Writing in the latter half of the Second Century, St Irenaeus of Lyons uses the corpus of Holy Scripture to expose Gnostic heretics:

> When, however, they are confuted from the Scriptures, they turn round and accuse these same Scriptures, as if they were not correct, nor of authority, and [assert] that they are

---

[34] St Luke xxiv.25-27
[35] St Luke xxiv.32
[36] FEF I, ¶268
[37] Synod of Rome (AD382) The Decree of Pope Damasus contains the Canon of Scripture, (Denzinger, 2012) p 70
[38] Council of Hippo AD393 Canon 36, (Akin, 2010) p 164 at which Landon claims St Augustine was present as a priest. (Landon, 1942?) (Entry under Council of Africa AD393)
[39] Council of Carthage AD397, (Denzinger, 2012) p 73, and Council of Carthage AD419. (Akin, 2010), p 165

> ambiguous, and that the truth cannot be extracted from them by those who are ignorant of tradition. For [they allege] that the truth was not delivered by means of written documents, but *vivâ voce*: wherefore also Paul declared, "But we speak wisdom among those that are perfect, but not the wisdom of this world."[40] And this wisdom each one of them alleges to be the fiction of his own inventing, forsooth; so that, according to their idea, the truth properly resides at one time in Valentinus, at another in Marcion, at another in Cerinthus, then afterwards in Basilides, or has even been indifferently in any other opponent, who could speak nothing pertaining to salvation. For every one of these men, being altogether of a perverse disposition, depraving the system of truth, is not ashamed to preach himself.[41]

It is clear that, a single century after the apostles, St Irenaeus is demonstrating that Holy Scripture is very much part of how the Church communicates her faith in order to teach catechumens and refute heretics and that rejection of Holy Scripture is regarded as a heresy.

The Place of Tradition

The Apostolic Fathers[42] who lived before any formal New Testament was ratified demonstrate that Holy Scripture does not exist *in vacuo* but rather within the context of a living community called the Church. Thus while Holy Scripture possesses a primacy of authority by virtue of its epistemic proximity to the life of Our Lord, the secondary witness of the Apostolic Fathers must be taken into account and the Tradition of the Church growing up alongside the New Testament is of great importance.

The "disciple" (Mathetes) expresses the importance of being true to divine revelation in his letter to Diognetes:

> For who that is rightly taught and begotten by the loving Word, would not seek to learn accurately the things which have been clearly shown by the Word to His disciples, to whom the Word being manifested has revealed them, speaking plainly [to them], not understood indeed by the unbelieving, but conversing with the disciples, who, being esteemed faithful by Him, acquired a knowledge of the

---

[40] I Corinthians ii.6
[41] St Irenaeus of Lyons, Against Heresies III, ii.1 (ANF I, p 415)
[42] See, for example, (Holmes, 2007) for how this term is understood.

> mysteries of the Father? For which reason He sent the Word, that He might be manifested to the world; and He, being despised by the people [of the Jews], was, when preached by the Apostles, believed on by the Gentiles. This is He who was from the beginning, who appeared as if new, and was found old, and yet who is ever born afresh in the hearts of the saints. This is He who, being from everlasting, is to-day called the Son; through whom the Church is enriched, and grace, widely spread, increases in the saints, furnishing understanding, revealing mysteries, announcing times, rejoicing over the faithful, giving to those that seek, by whom the limits of faith are not broken through, nor the boundaries set by the fathers passed over. Then the fear of the law is chanted, and the grace of the prophets is known, and the faith of the gospels is established, and the tradition of the Apostles is preserved, and the grace of the Church exults; which grace if you grieve not, you shall know those things which the Word teaches, by whom He wills, and when He pleases. For whatever things we are moved to utter by the will of the Word commanding us, we communicate to you with pains, and from a love of the things that have been revealed to us.[43]

There is no "seam" along which Scripture and Tradition are sewn, for Tradition must necessarily exist with Holy Scripture and *vice versa*. St Irenaeus, in refuting heretics, demonstrates the meaning of what we understand to be Tradition:

> But, again, when we refer them [i.e. Gnostic heretics] to that tradition which originates from the apostles, [and] which is preserved by means of the succession of presbyters in the Churches, they object to tradition, saying that they themselves are wiser not merely than the presbyters, but even than the apostles, because they have discovered the unadulterated truth. For [they maintain] that the apostles intermingled the things of the law with the words of the Saviour; and that not the apostles alone, but even the Lord Himself, spoke as at one time from the Demiurge, at another from the intermediate place, and yet again from the Pleroma, but that they themselves, indubitably, unsulliedly, and purely, have knowledge of the hidden mystery: this is, indeed, to blaspheme their Creator after a most impudent manner! It

---

[43] Epistle to Diognetes (c AD160) (ANF I p29)

comes to this, therefore, that these men do now consent neither to Scripture nor to tradition.[44]

As part of this Apostolic Tradition, St Paul is clear that he has taught the Corinthians much which he has received and bids them to transmit:

> Be ye followers of me, even as I also am of Christ. Now I praise you, brethren, that ye remember me in all things, and keep the ordinances, as I delivered them to you.[45]

And also to the Thessalonians:

> But we are bound to give thanks alway to God for you, brethren beloved of the Lord, because God hath from the beginning chosen you to salvation through sanctification of the Spirit and belief of the truth: Whereunto he called you by our gospel, to the obtaining of the glory of our Lord Jesus Christ. Therefore, brethren, stand fast, and hold the traditions which ye have been taught, whether by word, or our epistle.[46]

Apostolic Tradition is very much present alongside the Holy Scriptures and consonant with them because they are both centred on Our Lord, His calling and teaching and His active presence through His grace.

The Patristic Use of Reason

Likewise, the use of Reason to infer from both Scripture and Tradition is employed perhaps most obviously by St Paul in his address to the philosophers at the Areopagus.[47] By the second century, Bishop Melito of Sardis, known as "The Philosopher", in writing a lost apology to Marcus Aurelius refers to Christianity as a philosophy indicating that the use of philosophical reasoning was prevalent in discerning the Truth.[48] Tertullian famously exclaims:

> What indeed has Athens to do with Jerusalem? What concord is there between the Academy and the Church? What between heretics and Christians? Our instruction comes from the porch of Solomon, who had himself taught that the Lord

---

[44] St Irenaeus of Lyons, Against Heretics III, ii.2 (ANF I, p415)
[45] I Corinthians xi.2
[46] II Thessalonians ii.13-15
[47] Acts xvii.22-31
[48] ANF VIII, p 750

> should be sought in simplicity of heart. Away with all attempts to produce a mottled Christianity of Stoic, Platonic, and dialectic composition! We want no curious disputation after possessing Christ Jesus, no inquisition after enjoying the gospel! With our faith, we desire no further belief. For this is our palmary faith, that there is nothing which we ought to believe besides.[49]

Yet, his concern is about pagan philosophy especially "unhappy Aristotle" and one might be persuaded that, given his later Montanist tendencies, this is somewhat of an overreaction, after all, "The mouth of the righteous speaketh wisdom, and his tongue talketh of judgment."[50] Wisdom has its origins in God: she, herself, says:

> I lead in the way of righteousness, in the midst of the paths of judgment: That I may cause those that love me to inherit substance; and I will fill their treasures. The LORD possessed me in the beginning of his way, before his works of old. I was set up from everlasting, from the beginning, or ever the earth was. When there were no depths, I was brought forth; when there were no fountains abounding with water.[51]

Reason based on righteousness, i.e. God and His revelation to us, is used profusely by St Justin Martyr, Origen, St Augustine, St John Chrysostom who succeed the Apostolic Fathers in the subsequent centuries. Thus the method of simple deduction from Scripture and Tradition is to be seen as authoritative especially when ratified by the truly Oecumenical Councils, i.e. those whose canons, dogmata and decretals are accepted by the Catholic Church. This point will be explored further below in terms of the Cyrillic-Vincentian Catholicity.

Given that the Eastern Church and the Western Church separated from each other in a gradual disenfranchisement known as the Great Schism, and somewhat arbitrarily dated at 1054, the loss of the conversation between the two branches of the Church renders the differences in Tradition less authoritative and more speculative: how can a council be Oecumenical if half of the Church refuses to recognise its authority? It is here that ambiguities lie and need further examination in the light of the doctrine that the Church receives before this Schism. Nonetheless, given the agreement between the Roman Catholic Church and the Eastern Orthodox on the matter, it can be said that there are truly Seven Oecumenical councils even if

---

[49] Tertullian, Prescription against Heretics vii, (ANF III, p 246)
[50] Psalm xxxvii.30
[51] Proverbs viii.20-24

the criteria for what constitutes an Oecumenical Council are rather vague and disputed.

For modern Christians, there is a temptation to read into the Gospel an acceptance of a point of view which is largely inspired by the ambient culture. As will be seen in the discussion of matters of Anglican heritage, culture is the way that Christians express themselves in their age but, if culture is allowed to dictate what Christian doctrine says, the centrality and eternity of the Gospel becomes subordinate to that culture and not to the Eternal Person of Our Lord Jesus Christ. How does the modern Christian know that he is indeed preaching the right Gospel?

According to the Whole

There follows from this the question of what Catholicism really means. The Greek word καθολικος (from κατα + όλον) literally means "according to the whole."

St Ignatius of Antioch

The word "Catholic" has its earliest existing statement in a letter by St Ignatius of Antioch (c 35 – c108):

> See that ye all follow the bishop, even as Jesus Christ does the Father, and the presbytery as ye would the apostles; and reverence the deacons, as being the institution of God. Let no man do anything connected with the Church without the bishop. Let that be deemed a proper Eucharist, which is [administered] either by the bishop, or by one to whom he has entrusted it. Wherever the bishop shall appear, there let the multitude [of the people] also be; even as, wherever Jesus Christ is, there is the Catholic (καθολικὴ) Church. It is not lawful without the bishop either to baptize or to celebrate a love-feast; but whatsoever he shall approve of, that is also pleasing to God, so that everything that is done may be secure and valid.[52]

It should be noted, first, that St Ignatius writes as if the word "Catholic" has been in use for some time and this is written in the first half of the Second Century. It does seem to suggest that the word is associated with the church from a very early point in its history. Second, it is to be noticed that the notion of sacramental validity[53] is

---

[52] St Ignatius of Antioch, Letter to the Smyrnaeans, viii (ANF I, p 89)
[53] St Ignatius uses the word βεβαιον ((Holmes, 2007) p 256) meaning "firm" or "sound" and which is translated as "valid".

inherent in the episcopal celebration of the Eucharist and Baptism. While the Eucharist becomes delegated to the priesthood and Baptism to potentially any human being, it is in unity with the bishop that these sacraments have their effect.

It is also to be noticed that, according to St Ignatius, there is no mention of the Pope (i.e. the Bishop of Rome) in his understanding of Catholicism nor of Rome. This is also true of other early texts which speak of the Catholic Church.[54] This is where Anglican Catholics first see the idea of being Catholic as not exclusive to being in communion with the Bishop of Rome, however desirable that may be. While it is understood that Roman Catholicism is not the defining principle of Catholicism, Anglican Catholics recognise the Pope as their patriarch[55] and hope that, one day, they may once more be seen to be in the same communion as he.

St Cyril of Jerusalem

St Cyril of Jerusalem (313-386) explains to those entering the Church what Catholic Church means:

> It is called Catholic then because it extends over all the world, from one end of the earth to the other; and because it teaches universally and completely one and all the doctrines which ought to come to men's knowledge, concerning things both visible and invisible, heavenly and earthly; and because it brings into subjection to godliness the whole race of mankind, governors and governed, learned and unlearned; and because it universally treats and heals the whole class of sins, which are committed by soul or body, and possesses in itself every form of virtue which is named, both in deeds and words, and in every kind of spiritual gifts.
>
> And it is rightly named ἐκκλησία because it calls forth and assembles together all men; according as the Lord says in Leviticus, And make an assembly for all the congregation at the door of the tabernacle of witness. And it is to be noted, that the word assemble, is used for the first time in the Scriptures here, at the time when the Lord puts Aaron into the High-priesthood. And in Deuteronomy also the Lord says to Moses, Assemble the people unto Me, and let them hear My words, that they may learn to fear Me. And he again mentions the name of the Church, when he says concerning the Tables, And

---

[54] See, for example, The Martyrdom of St Polycarp xix, The Muratorian Fragment, Tertullian's Prescription against Heretics xxx, and Canons VIII and XIX of the First Council of Nicaea
[55] Despite Pope Benedict XVI's rejection of the title "Patriarch of the West".

> on them were written all the words which the Lord spoke with you in the mount out of the midst of the fire in the day of the Assembly; as if he had said more plainly, in the day in which you were called and gathered together by God. The Psalmist also says, I will give thanks unto You, O Lord, in the great Congregation; I will praise You among much people.[56]

Again, in this extract, nothing can be seen about the office of the Pope defining what it means to be Catholic: it appears that the word predates the papal office as we now understand it. Indeed, we notice that St Cyril interprets St Matthew xvi.18 to mean that all Christians participate in the building of the Church with St Peter. Indeed,

> Bishop Lightfoot (Ignatius, ad Smyrnæos, viii.) traces the original and later senses of the word "Catholic" very fully. "In its earliest usages, therefore, as a fluctuating epithet of ἐκκλησία, 'catholic' means 'universal,' as opposed to 'individual,' 'particular.' In its later sense, as a fixed attribute, it implies orthodoxy as opposed to heresy, conformity as opposed to dissent." Commenting on this passage of Cyril, the Bishop adds that "these two latter reasons, that it (the Church) is comprehensive in doctrine, and that it is universal in application, can only be regarded as secondary glosses."[57]

Bishop Lightfoot suggests that there are two definitions of "Catholic", an earlier one as found with St Ignatius meaning "universal" as opposed to "particular" and a later as found with St Cyril with it meaning "orthodox" and "conformity" and that the latter definition is in some way inferior to the first. The question that remains with Lightfoot's conclusion is how the first definition as "universal" is to be achieved without the second. How can the particular become the universal without some unifying principle? St Ignatius says it clearly, to wit, "wherever Jesus Christ is, there is the Catholic Church."

This cannot be a unifying maxim in just a single sentence. Moslems and Christians are both monotheist religions but they are not the same religion – belief in God is not enough to render them anything other than particular monotheist religions. Likewise, many men have claimed to be Jesus Christ but have taught remarkably different things, thus even the name "Jesus Christ" is insufficient in itself to generate a fellowship. The Jesus Christ meant by St Ignatius must refer to the Divine Logos found in Holy Scriptures and carried by the Tradition of the Church. Aside from a fellowship which renders Lightfoot's particulars into a universal, there must be some

---

[56] St Cyril of Jerusalem Catechetical Lecture XVIII.xxiii-xxiv, (NPNF2 VII, p 139-140)
[57] *Ibid.*, Footnote 6

universal principle which prevents congregations from being particular. St Cyril's definition of "Catholic" must be the principle that causes St Ignatius' definition of "Catholic".

Dr Ludwig Ott agrees:

> The Church is called Catholic especially on account of her spatial extent, that is, on account of her extension over the whole earth. We may distinguish Virtual Catholicity, that is, the intention to extend over the whole earth, together with the capacity to achieve that purpose, and Actual Catholicity, that is, the actual extension of the Church over the whole earth. Virtual Catholicity existed from the beginning; Actual Catholicity, by its nature, could only be achieved after a fairly long historical development. Actual Catholicity is said to be physical if it embraces all peoples of the earth, even if not all individual men, and moral if it includes only the greater part of them. Catholicity, of course, presupposes unity.[58]

Unity of mind is explicit in St Paul's understanding to the Church. In the letter to the Church in Ephesus, he writes:

> I therefore, the prisoner of the Lord, beseech you that ye walk worthy of the vocation wherewith ye are called, With all lowliness and meekness, with longsuffering, forbearing one another in love; Endeavouring to keep the unity of the Spirit in the bond of peace. There is one body, and one Spirit, even as ye are called in one hope of your calling; One Lord, one faith, one baptism, One God and Father of all, who is above all, and through all, and in you all.[59]

While St Ignatius does not explicitly say so, it is eminently reasonable to infer that his understanding of Catholicism is the same as St Cyril's Catholicism and thus the latter is an essential part rather than a "secondary gloss".

St Vincent and his Canon

Through the words of St Cyril, it can be seen that the Catholic Religion is an holistic religion in that it binds all people scattered throughout the space-time continuum

---

[58] (Ott, 1952) p306, §17
[59] Ephesians iv.1-6

through a common acceptance of Christian orthodoxy (Cyrillic-Vincentian Catholicism) which enables orthopraxis and *orthokoinōnia* (Ignatian Catholicism).

A fundamental idea of what it is to be Catholic is expressed by St Vincent of Lerins (d. 450) which encapsulates how God intends His Gospel to be spread:

> But here some one perhaps will ask, Since the canon of Scripture is complete, and sufficient of itself for everything, and more than sufficient, what need is there to join with it the authority of the Church's interpretation? For this reason—because, owing to the depth of Holy Scripture, all do not accept it in one and the same sense, but one understands its words in one way, another in another; so that it seems to be capable of as many interpretations as there are interpreters. For Novatian expounds it one way, Sabellius another, Donatus another, Arius, Eunomius, Macedonius, another, Photinus, Apollinaris, Priscillian, another, Iovinian, Pelagius, Celestius, another, lastly, Nestorius another. Therefore, it is very necessary, on account of so great intricacies of such various error, that the rule for the right understanding of the prophets and apostles should be framed in accordance with the standard of Ecclesiastical and Catholic interpretation.
>
> Moreover, in the Catholic Church itself, all possible care must be taken, that we hold that faith which has been believed everywhere, always, by all. For that is truly and in the strictest sense Catholic, which, as the name itself and the reason of the thing declare, comprehends all universally. This rule we shall observe if we follow universality, antiquity, consent. We shall follow universality if we confess that one faith to be true, which the whole Church throughout the world confesses; antiquity, if we in no wise depart from those interpretations which it is manifest were notoriously held by our holy ancestors and fathers; consent, in like manner, if in antiquity itself we adhere to the consentient definitions and determinations of all, or at the least of almost all priests and doctors.[60]

St Vincent makes a substantial list of all those heretics who have tried to pervert the Christian Faith to meet their own philosophies. Then, he makes it very clear: the Catholic faith is that "which has been believed everywhere, always, by all" – *quod ubique, quod semper, quod ab omnibus creditum est*. He is writing after the third

---

[60] St Vincent of Lerins: Commonitorium II.5-6, (NPNF2, XI, p 132)

Oecumenical Council of Ephesus and thus is quite clear about the impact of an Oecumenical Council on the Catholic Church.

Prudence is necessary in interpreting this canon. Thomas Guarino[61] makes it clear that a church that St Vincent might describe as ancient is not part of some mythic golden age but rather that Tradition is living process but which hardens like magma from a volcano or toughens like bark on a tree. Our understanding of the Catholic Faith grows like a child into a man, but it is possible to discern in the child the features present in the adult. No doctrine satisfies the Vincentian Canon in its literal interpretation, but there is a clear principle to be had within the spirit of its interpretation. To discern this spirit of how it is to be interpreted, one must apply some logic.

The Reflexivity of the Vincentian Canon[62]

We see that St Vincent has produced a general statement, and general statements have to apply generally.

If "only physical evidence determines the truth" then where is the physical evidence which will determine the truth of that statement? If there is no such thing as Absolute Truth, then is the statement "there is no Absolute Truth" an absolute truth or not? The question is, therefore, does the Vincentian Canon satisfy the Vincentian Canon? Can it be said that the words of his Commonitorium have been believed everywhere, always, by all – i.e. does it possess universality, antiquity and consent? If this can be done, then the Vincentian Canon becomes a self-consistent definition of Catholicism and a criterion by which one can test for Catholicism. It also demonstrates a coherent reasonableness inherent within Catholic thought which is consonant with Man as a creature that God intends to be a thinking creature. If not, then the Vincentian Canon possesses no evidence to be part of the Catholic Faith and this undermines the weight of Catholic authority. If Arianism fails the Vincentian Canon, then there is legitimate doubt that Arianism is Catholic. The problem arises if the Vincentian Canon fails the Vincentian Canon.

Fortunately, it seems from the Commonitorium that St Vincent is setting up the basis upon which the Orthodox Churches understand the Faith. It has also been shown in the Introduction above[63] that Holy Scripture requires a unity of Faith, Lord and Baptism. St Paul exhorts universality and consent:

---

[61] (Guarino, 2013) p 41-42
[62] This section is an expansion of the author's weblog post, the original of which may be found at https://warwickensis.blogspot.com/2014/01/reflexive-catholicism.html
[63] Ephesians iv.1-6

> Now I beseech you, brethren, by the name of our Lord Jesus Christ, that ye all speak the same thing, and that there be no divisions among you; but that ye be perfectly joined together in the same mind and in the same judgment.[64]

and antiquity:

> Moreover, brethren, I declare unto you the gospel which I preached unto you, which also ye have received, and wherein ye stand; By which also ye are saved, if ye keep in memory what I preached unto you, unless ye have believed in vain. For I delivered unto you first of all that which I also received, how that Christ died for our sins according to the scriptures;[65]

And St Luke begins his Gospel with the intention of going back to the beginning of Christian testimony:

> Forasmuch as many have taken in hand to set forth in order a declaration of those things which are most surely believed among us, Even as they delivered them unto us, which from the beginning were eyewitnesses, and ministers of the word; It seemed good to me also, having had perfect understanding of all things from the very first, to write unto thee in order, most excellent Theophilus, That thou mightest know the certainty of those things, wherein thou hast been instructed.[66]

The Vincentian Canon may thus be shown to be consonant with Holy Scripture which itself possesses universality, antiquity and consent.

Further, the whole point of an Oecumenical Council is for the Bishops from all around the world to gather together in order to find consensus on matters of Faith in order to preserve the Faith and promulgate it into all territories. Thus in an Oecumenical Council, we have *quod ubique* in the gathering of the world's bishops and the congregations that accept the teaching of the Council, the *quod semper* in their intention to find and preserve the "faith which was once delivered unto the saints" in a consensus that conveys that *quod ubique* to all believers in order to produce the *quod ab omnibus*. Thus we see that it is very much the *raison d'être* of the Oecumenical Council to corroborate the Vincentian Canon. If the Councils are

---

[64] I Corinthians i.10
[65] I Corinthians xv.1-3
[66] St Luke i.1-4

thus Catholic then so is the Vincentian Canon: thus it can be regarded as a proper universal statement and thus not self-refuting.

This might be regarded by some as an exercise in raising futility or tautology to a high art; however, it does actually demonstrate the reliability of St Vincent's definition of "Catholic" as something the Early Church understood before it was thus phrased and as something accepted afterwards. This definition can be accepted in good Faith. It means that any Church that accepts the doctrine of the Seven Oecumenical Councils of the Undivided Church is truly Catholic in principle. That the Vincentian Canon produces a tautology is not insignificant but rather a great comfort.

The fact that there are two "Eighth Oecumenical" Councils both in Constantinople – the Western being that of 869-870 and the Eastern being 879-880 which directly contradict each other[67] – demonstrates that neither is truly a Catholic Council in the Cyrillic-Vincentian sense and the subsequent Schism renders further claims to being Oecumenical moot on the grounds of consent and universality.

The self-consistency of the Vincentian Canon also means that weaker definitions that have been promulgated since then can be effectively ruled out. "Catholic" cannot mean "all-inclusive" because that would mean that it could include atheists and other religions which is inconsonant with Scripture:

> Verily, verily, I say unto you, He that entereth not by the door into the sheepfold, but climbeth up some other way, the same is a thief and a robber.[68]
>
> I am the door: by me if any man enter in, he shall be saved, and shall go in and out, and find pasture.[69]

That is certainly not to say that non-Christians are irredeemable. Indeed, if the prayers of the Church at Mass are answered then the possibility does exist if not the actuality. For, at the offering of the Chalice, the prayer is said, "that it may ascend as a sweet-smelling savour for our salvation and for that of the whole world."[70] However, redemption can only come through Our Lord Jesus Christ as the Mass makes very clear.

What the Vincentian Canon compels the Church to do is to evaluate each statement made by the saints on its own merit. No one saint is infallible. Just because a Church

---

[67] See (Landon, 1942?) I, p215-219
[68] St John x.1
[69] St John x.9
[70] The English Missal offertory prayers.

Father's name can be attached to a statement does not render it Christian Doctrine automatically. The opinions of one person cannot rule the Church, even if that name is St Augustine of Hippo especially as evidenced by his controversial doctrine of Limbo which the Roman Catholic Church has recently rejected and the Eastern Orthodox never held. The Church is bound to recognise the voice of God within the utterances of those who seek the Truth despite being able to be incorrect. St Vincent's idea that the Church of the present should be recognisable in the Church of the past in the same way that a man is recognisable from his baby photographs shows that Christian doctrine is not a matter of a popular vote. The Oecumenical Councils were not Parish Church Council meetings subject to the vicissitudes and caprice of those with their own agenda, but rather a striving for the Truth that has always been in evidence within the Church.

Finally, it may be seen that the Catholicity of the Vincentian allows the Continuing Anglican Movement to make the statement:

> We acknowledge that rule of faith laid down by St. Vincent of Lerins: Let us hold that which has been believed everywhere, always and by all, for that is truly and properly Catholic.[71]

A Note on Reason

Care must be taken in understanding the authoritative nature of Reason. It was through use of a certain type of reasoning that resulted in burning heretics alive at the stake in the belief that the burning of the flesh would purify the spirit.[72] Yet, it is by careful reasoning from Holy Scripture and Tradition that the full realisation of the Holy Trinity is discovered: One God in Three persons.

Dianoia

Writing in the Church of England after the Reformation, Fr Richard Hooker (1554-1600) discusses the "Law of Reason" being the laws of right reason that normatively govern Christian conduct.

> Be it in matter of the one kind or of the other, what Scripture doth plainly deliver, to that the first place both of credit and obedience is due; the next whereunto is whatsoever any man

---

[71] The Affirmation of St Louis, Preface
[72] See the (Great Courses) Course Notes by Professor Daniel Robinson for The Great Ideas of Philosophy, Lecture 24: "Let us burn witches to save them." See also C Larner, Witchcraft and Religion, Blackwell 1984, and B. Levack, The Witch-Hunt in Early Modern Europe, Longman, 1995.

> can necessarily conclude by force of reason; after this the Church succeedeth that which the Church by her ecclesiastical authority shall probably think and define to be true or good, must in congruity of reason overrule all other inferior judgments whatsoever.[73]

What is meant by Reason here? The Greek word is διάνοια - *dianoia* which literally means something passing through the mind, διά + νοῦς i.e. "through" or directed thinking. It was Plato who termed it to mean the use of the intellect to understand things and draw conclusions.[74]

Our Lord says, "Thou shalt love the Lord thy God with all thy heart, and with all thy soul, and with all thy mind (διανοίᾳ)."[75] With all that is reasonable within the soul, in all decision making processes, Man is to seek after God. This does show that this Reason can be led astray. Indeed, this is seen so much in Holy Scripture.

Our Lady sings that God "hath scattered the proud in the imagination (διανοίᾳ) of their hearts."[76] Twice in his letter to the Ephesians, St Paul uses the term *dianoia* negatively.

> And you hath he quickened, who were dead in trespasses and sins; Wherein in time past ye walked according to the course of this world, according to the prince of the power of the air, the spirit that now worketh in the children of disobedience: Among whom also we all had our conversation in times past in the lusts of our flesh, fulfilling the desires of the flesh and of the mind (διανοιῶν) and were by nature the children of wrath, even as others.[77]

> This I say therefore, and testify in the Lord, that ye henceforth walk not as other Gentiles walk, in the vanity of their mind, Having the understanding (διανοίᾳ) darkened, being alienated from the life of God through the ignorance that is in them, because of the blindness of their heart: Who being past feeling have given themselves over unto lasciviousness, to work all uncleanness with greediness.[78]

---

[73] Richard Hooker , The Laws of Ecclesiastical Polity, Book 5.VIII.2
[74] See his reasoning on the Divided Line in the Republic (Rep 6.509d–6.511e; 7.533c–7.534b)
[75] St Matthew xxii.37, c.f. also St Mark xii.30
[76] The Magnificat (St Luke i.51)
[77] Ephesians ii.3
[78] Ephesians iv.17-19

And in the letter to the Colossians, he says,

> For it pleased the Father that in him should all fulness dwell; And, having made peace through the blood of his cross, by him to reconcile all things unto himself; by him, I say, whether they be things in earth, or things in heaven. And you, that were sometime alienated and enemies in your mind (διανοίᾳ) by wicked works, yet now hath he reconciled In the body of his flesh through death, to present you holy and unblameable and unreproveable in his sight: If ye continue in the faith grounded and settled, and be not moved away from the hope of the gospel, which ye have heard, and which was preached to every creature which is under heaven;[79]

Clearly, human reasoning is easily led astray, and it is in fact led astray by what is already in the human heart.

> There is a way which seemeth right unto a man, but the end thereof are the ways of death.[80]

And St Paul will say that this is because the "wages of sin is death".[81] Human nature is broken[82] and this affects our thinking, too.

A More Positive View

As has been shown in the use of Reason in the Apostolic Fathers, God values human reasoning abilities, otherwise why would He have bestowed them upon His creation? If St Thomas Aquinas is told by the Lord, "thou hast written well of me"[83] then Reason is something which, when based on the Truth, expresses the Truth.

> And we know that the Son of God is come, and hath given us an understanding (διάνοιαν), that we may know him that is true, and we are in him that is true, even in his Son Jesus Christ. This is the true God, and eternal life.[84]

---

[79] Colossians i.19-23
[80] Proverbs xiv.12
[81] Romans vi.23
[82] Romans v.12
[83] Raïssa Maritain, tr Julie Kernan, The Angel of the Schools, Longmans, Green and Co. New York Toronto 1942
[84] I John v.20

Twice God speaks in the letter to the Hebrews about the New Covenant that will refresh the mind.

> For this is the covenant that I will make with the house of Israel after those days, saith the Lord; I will put my laws into their mind (διάνοιαν), and write them in their hearts: and I will be to them a God, and they shall be to me a people:[85]

God encourages human beings to use the ability to think, reason and deduce but it is clear that, if the authority of reason is to be used to make good clear deductions about God, then those deductions need to be started by God, grounded in God and affirmed by God. St Justin Martyr says:

But both Him, and the Son (who came forth from Him and taught us these things, and the host of the other good angels who follow and are made like to Him), and the prophetic Spirit, we worship and adore, knowing them in reason and truth, and declaring without grudging to every one who wishes to learn, as we have been taught.[86]

The psalmist says, "Wherewithal shall a young man cleanse his way: even by ruling himself after thy word."[87] St Peter says,

> Wherefore gird up the loins of your mind (διανοίας), be sober, and hope to the end for the grace that is to be brought unto you at the revelation of Jesus Christ;[88]

Yet, while Reason is a source of authority in the Church, it can only ever be bound tightly with Scripture and Tradition. Hooker did not invent the analogy of Anglican thought being a three legged-stool based on legs representing Tradition, Scripture and Reason. It is a wrong analogy as it has the implication that the three legs are of equal length and thus equal weight. This is not true. A better analogy would be three stones resting one on top of the other. The bottom stone is Holy Scripture upon which Tradition has its base and on top is Reason resting on all three.[89] Even then, this is somewhat disingenuous since, again, no two can be separated from each

---

[85] Hebrews viii.10 and c.f. Hebrews x.16
[86] St Justin Martyr, First Apology vi (ANF I, p164)
[87] Psalm cix.9.
[88] I Peter i.13
[89] Canon Robert S. Munday, Three-Legged Stool of Anglicanism, https://virtueonline.org/three-legged-stool-anglicanism-robert-s-munday

other: there is no apparent stratification but rather a continuum of Catholic Authority.

The Oecumenical Councils were the result of Reason being used and so it is clear that Reason has its pride of place within the Catholic Faith but at a much less authoritative place than either of the other two sources of authority. In effect, Reason is learned to be Right through Scripture and Tradition and this renders Right Reason really as being a part of Tradition since, when Reason is shown to be Right, it becomes part of the received Tradition. This demonstrates the organic nature of the Principles of Catholic Authority.

A Note on Experience

Another problem presents itself in a certain modern tendency to bring Catholic Doctrine "up-to-date".

Spong and Schori

As a prime example of how modernistic thought misleads Christians, one might look at the writings of John Shelby Spong, especially A New Christianity for a New World (Bravo 2003). Another good example is that of ECUSA's Presiding Bishop Katherine Jefferts Schori whose body of preaching contains some dubious theology, such as:

> Paul is annoyed at the slave girl. She's telling the same truth Paul and others claim for themselves. But Paul is annoyed, perhaps for being put in his place, and he responds by depriving her of her gift of spiritual awareness. Paul can't abide something he won't see as beautiful or holy, so he tries to destroy it.[90]

For both these Episcopalian Bishops, the modern worldview seems to have a greater authority than that of Holy Scripture.

The Catholic Church believes in the Communion of the Saints,[91] though it is better to make an examination of that as an aspect of Ignatian Catholicism below rather than Cyrillic-Vincentian. The Communion of the Saints encapsulates the whole Church, past, present, and future. Thus any change in doctrine would break that communion with the very saints who not only believed that doctrine but who lived, suffered and died to pass on that teaching of the Church. The Apostles suffered and

---

[90] Sermon at the 2009 General Convention and based on Acts xvi.16-34
[91] The Apostles' Creed

all but one (St John) died (Benedict XVI, 2007) proclaiming the bodily resurrection of Our Lord which is denied by Spong.

> Resurrection is an action of God. Jesus was raised into the meaning of God. Resurrection, therefore, cannot be a physical resuscitation occurring inside human history...
>
> I believe the resurrection of Jesus was real. I do not believe it has anything to do with an empty tomb or a resuscitated body. It is a vision of one not bound by any of the limitations of our humanity. It is a call into a new level of consciousness, a call into a new reality beyond time and space.[92]

One thing that to which all the Gospel witnesses attest is that the tomb was empty.[93] Further, Jesus is physically risen,[94] and thus, for Spong to justify his claim, he must reject the witness of Holy Scripture. Further, the Council of Ephesus ratified St Cyril of Alexandria's anathema against Nestorius.

> Whosoever shall not recognize that the Word of God suffered in the flesh, that he was crucified in the flesh, and that likewise in that same flesh he tasted death and that he has become the first-begotten of the dead, for, as he is God, he is the life and it is he that gives life: let him be anathema.[95]

In the same Council, St Cyril states clearly that the Catholic Faith has antiquity and that those who try to change it put themselves in grave peril:

> As this letter of the most reverend and pious Capreolus, bishop of Carthage, which has been read, contains a most lucid expression of opinion, let it be inserted in the Acts. For it wishes that the ancient dogmas of the faith should be confirmed, and that novelties, absurdly conceived and impiously brought forth, should be reprobated and proscribed.[96]

To which the assembled bishops cry:

---

[92] Point 7 in A Call for a New Reformation, The Fourth R, Volume 11-4, July-August 1998.
[93] St Matthew xxviii.6; St Mark xvi.6; St Luke xxiv.3; St John xx.5-7;
[94] St Luke xxiv.36-43, especially v36; St John xx.19-29
[95] Twelfth Anathema in the Council of Ephesus (NPNF2, XIV, p 217)
[96] From Session I of the Council of Ephesus (NPNF2,XIV, p 218)

> These are the sentiments of all of us, these are the things we all say — the accomplishment of this is the desire of us all.[97]

What we see here is how Holy Scripture and Holy Tradition together reject Spong's hypothesis and declare him to be clearly outside the Catholic Faith.

With regards to Bishop Schori, in Acts xvi, St Paul is arrested for driving the spirit of divination (πνεῦμα Πύθωνος) out of the girl (v16) which releases her from servitude to a master (as explicitly stated in v 16). This arrest is then responsible for the salvation of Paul's gaoler and his whole household (v33). This rather contradicts Schori's view of the events. The plain reading of Holy Scripture alone is enough to demonstrate that she is preaching an innovation unsupported by Catholic principles. St Augustine demonstrates how the text from the Acts of the Apostles is to be read:

> For though the ghost of the dead Samuel foretold the truth to King Saul, that does not make such sacrilegious observances as those by which his ghost was brought up the less detestable; and though the ventriloquist woman in the Acts of the Apostles bore true testimony to the apostles of the Lord, the Apostle Paul did not spare the evil spirit on that account, but rebuked and cast it out, and so made the woman clean.[98]

St Irenaeus makes an allusion to the text to demonstrate the heresy of Marcus who uses a familiar spirit,[99] and St John Chrysostom, too, in his commentary on the Acts of the Apostles recognises that this spirit is infernal in its nature:

> Say, what is this demon? The god, as they call him, Python: from the place he is so called. Do you mark that Apollo also is a demon? And (the demon) wished to bring them into temptation: (therefore) to provoke them, the same followed Paul and us, and cried, saying, These men are the servants of the most high God, which show unto us the way of salvation.[100]

Apostolic Experience

It must be stated that an undeniable fact is that the Holy Scriptures, the Tradition and the use of Reason have their origin in the personal experiences of a few

---

[97] *Ibid.*
[98] St Augustine of Hippo, On Christian Doctrine II, xxiii (NPNF1, II, p547)
[99] St Irenaeus of Lyons, Against Heresies I, xiii.3 (ANF I, p334)
[100] St John Chrysostom, Homily XXXV on the Acts of the Apostles (Recapitulation) (NPNF 1, XI, p 221)

individuals who are fortunate enough to come into contact with the Risen Christ at the time of His Resurrection. The question that needs to be addressed is to what extent individual religious experience can become Catholic Doctrine. The experience of the Fathers of the Church itself is founded upon the Rock of the Catholic Faith.[101]

There are modern theologians today who would like to make Experience the fourth source of authority alongside Scripture, Tradition, and Reason. Famously, Rev. John Wesley believes that truth reflects itself in the lives of men, not as individuals but collectively. He says that one recognises the truth when our eyes are open to it like the blind man who says, "Whether he be a sinner or no, I know not: one thing I know, that, whereas I was blind, now I see." [102] Of course, the blind man does have a unique position in that he comes face to face with the Lord Jesus and receives his sight. His experience is his Gospel.[103] This is undeniable. St Paul, too, receives his Gospel by his experience on the Damascus road – an experience he recounts several times[104] as proof of the sincerity of his conviction.

The main trouble is that this sort of conviction of "experience" is completely insufficient on its own. This sort of experience which, unsupported by Scripture, Tradition, or Reason leads to the sort of cults that we see all over the place.[105] In contrast, Christians take the many eye-witness statements about the person of Jesus Christ, His public addresses, His death and resurrection as a matter of faith based on good evidence in accordance with St John's exhortation to "believe not every spirit, but try the spirits whether they are of God: because many false prophets are gone out into the world."

Indeed, the Prophet Jeremiah proclaims the words of God about putting human authority before that which God reveals to us:

> Thus saith the LORD; Cursed be the man that trusteth in man, and maketh flesh his arm, and whose heart departeth from the LORD. For he shall be like the heath in the desert, and shall not see when good cometh; but shall inhabit the parched places in the wilderness, in a salt land and not inhabited. Blessed is the man that trusteth in the LORD, and whose hope the LORD is. For he shall be as a tree planted by the waters, and that spreadeth out her roots by the river, and shall not see when heat cometh, but her leaf shall be green; and shall not be careful in the year of drought, neither shall cease from yielding

---

[101] St Matthew xvi.18
[102] Rev John Wesley, Letter to Dr Conyers Middleton, 4th January 1749
[103] St John ix.25
[104] Acts ix, Acts xxii and Acts xxvi as well as references to it in I Corinthians xv and Galatians i.
[105] Such as lone witnesses to angelic beings pointing out golden plates.

fruit. The heart is deceitful above all things, and desperately wicked: who can know it? I the LORD search the heart, I try the reins, even to give every man according to his ways, and according to the fruit of his doings.[106]

Experience in the Theological Science

It is clear that our experiences must always be tried against what is scriptural, traditional, and reasonable before we can trust that they are not false, and therefore truly of God. This does suggest that the experience that Wesley says is a proof of God's authority is actually not a proof at all, but a means of forming what would amount to the equivalent of a scientific hypothesis.

St John endorses this spiritual science when he says:

> Beloved, believe not every spirit, but try the spirits whether they are of God: because many false prophets are gone out into the world. Hereby know ye the Spirit of God: Every spirit that confesseth that Jesus Christ is come in the flesh is of God: And every spirit that confesseth not that Jesus Christ is come in the flesh is not of God: and this is that spirit of antichrist, whereof ye have heard that it should come; and even now already is it in the world.[107]

In Scientific inquiry, a question is posed – e.g. "is there such thing as gravity?" – and that hypothesis is tested using the authority of empirical and objective evidence – i.e. dropping things and observing their fall. In order to ensure that the individual experience does not lead astray, there must be a grounding in seeking first the Kingdom of God and His Righteousness.[108] On informing the conscience, St Isaiah the Solitary (fl 431) says,

> Let us stand firm in the fear of God, rigorously practicing the virtues and not giving our conscience cause to stumble. In the fear of God let us keep our attention fixed within ourselves, until our conscience achieves its freedom. Then there will be a union between it and us, and thereafter it will be our guardian, showing us each thing that we must uproot. But if we do not obey our conscience, it will abandon us and we shall fall into the hands of our enemies, who will never let us go. This is what our Lord taught us when He said: 'Come to an agreement with

---

[106] Jeremiah xvii.5-10
[107] I John iv.1-3
[108] C.f. St Matthew vi.33

> your adversary quickly while you are with him in the road, lest he hand you over to the judge, and the judge deliver you to the officer and you are cast into prison. The conscience is called an 'adversary' because it opposes us when we wish to carry out the desires of our flesh; and if we do not listen to our conscience, it delivers us into the hands of our enemies. [109]

St Augustine comments on St John's words:

> There remains then the test by which it is to be proved to be the Spirit of God. He has indeed set down a sign, and this, belike, difficult: let us see, however. We are to recur to that charity; it is that which teaches us, because it is the unction. However, what says he here? Prove the spirits, whether they be from God: because many false prophets have gone out into this world. Now there are all heretics and all schismatics. How then am I to prove the spirit?[110]

Any spirit sent by God will conform to the tests of faith which the Church has received from Our Lord Jesus Christ.

One further problem with the notion of Experience as an authority is the lack of an appropriate definition or consistent term that comes from Scripture or the Fathers. Although Wesley clearly sees experience as a collective method of discernment,[111] it still cannot escape being subjective or personal. While the Christian life is centred on engaging with God at the personal level,[112] we cannot rely on our own experience as being normative for other people around us.[113] Our experience is part of the mystery of our own subjective individuality and no-one else. That cannot be Catholic – it is the reverse of Catholic. A private revelation can only be binding on the individual who receives it.

---

[109] St Isaiah the Solitary, On guarding the intellect: Twenty-seven texts, no. 3 (Various, 1979) I, p 22-23
[110] St Augustine, Homily on the Gospel of St John and his First Epistle VI.12 (NPNF1 VII, p 499)
[111] Rev John Wesley, Letter to Dr Conyers Middleton, 4th January 1749. Indeed, in that letter and in a most learned fashion, Wesley calls on Holy Scripture and the Church Fathers as well as reason to make his point against Dr Middleton's attack on the Church Fathers.
[112] i.e. seeking first the kingdom of God and His righteousness.
[113] Again, one might look at the examples of Bishops Spong and Schori.

The Necessity of Experience

This is not to say that Experience has no value – quite the opposite. Clearly the Catholic Faith came about by the experience of people who found God. Their experience becomes authoritative solely through the presence in Time of Our Lord Jesus Christ. His teaching does not change, but it can be expressed in diverse ways.

St Hermas (1st Century) receives a vision of an old woman and six young men building a tower.

> She said to me, Lo! Do you not see opposite to you a great tower, built upon the waters, of splendid square stones? For the tower was built square by those six young men who had come with her. But myriads of men were carrying stones to it, some dragging them from the depths, others removing them from the land, and they handed them to these six young men. They were taking them and building; and those of the stones that were dragged out of the depths, they placed in the building just as they were: for they were polished and fitted exactly into the other stones, and became so united one with another that the lines of juncture could not be perceived. And in this way the building of the tower looked as if it were made out of one stone.[114]

The Tower is the Church, the men are angels. The stones suffer different fates, but all build the Church up. When the tower is complete, the end will come.

It might be tempting to say that the time of miracles and visions is past. Yet, that is limiting the power of God. St Benedict performed many miracles, as did St Francis of Assisi, and in the twentieth century, there is the figure of Saint Pio of Pietrelcina, a stigmatic and mystic. Even today, there are reports of the Holy Fire that appears on the candles held by the Patriarch of Jerusalem every Holy Saturday.

It is right to be wary of anyone who comes to us and says, "Thus says the Lord…" for God is not a God of confusion.[115] The Catholic Faith never changes because the object of that faith never changes – One Lord, One Faith, One Baptism. Throughout His ministry, Our Lord shows how that Faith is already present in the Old Testament, how men have perverted it, and how He fulfils it in the New Testament.

---

[114] St Hermas, The Shepherd I. Vision Third.ii (ANF II, p 13)
[115] I Corinthians xiv.33

The Holy Ghost and the Unity of the Faith

Central to all of this relationship between subjective experience and the objective reality of God is the Holy Ghost, for it is in the work of the Holy Ghost that faith has its beginning. St John says:

> But the Comforter, which is the Holy Ghost, whom the Father will send in my name, he shall teach you all things, and bring all things to your remembrance, whatsoever I have said unto you.[116]

Based on this, William Lane Craig points out that the very basic belief that the Christian possesses is directly and interpersonally from the Holy Ghost:

> Now the truth that the Holy Spirit teaches us is not, I'm convinced, the subtleties of Christian doctrine. There are too many Spirit-filled Christians who differ doctrinally for that to be the case. What John is talking about is the inner assurance the Holy Spirit gives of the basic truths of the Christian faith… This assurance does not come from human arguments but directly from the Holy Spirit himself.[117]

Craig's reasoning resonates with the Church Fathers. St John Chrysostom says, "I show that the Apostles received nothing in writing, but received [it] in their hearts through the Holy Ghost. Wherefore also Christ said, When He comes, He will bring all things to your remembrance, and He shall teach you."[118] Likewise, the individual Christian receives the Holy Ghost guiding him into all truth:

> Further, Esaias the prophet is ordered to take "a new book, and write in it"[119] certain things: the Spirit prophesying that through the exposition of the Scriptures there would come afterwards the sacred knowledge, which at that period was still unwritten, because not yet known. For it was spoken from the beginning to those only who understand. Now that the Saviour has taught the apostles, the unwritten rendering of the written [Scripture] has been handed down also to us,

---

[116] St John xiv.26
[117] (Craig, 2008) p 44.
[118] St John Chrysostom, Homily XIV on the Epistle to the Hebrews, v (NPNF1 XIV p 435)
[119] Isaiah viii.1.

> inscribed by the power of God on hearts new, according to the renovation of the book.[120]

And, by conversing directly and interpersonally, the Holy Spirit gives each individual Christian no little comfort that their salvation is in the hands of God.

> The Spirit itself beareth witness with our spirit, that we are the children of God: And if children, then heirs; heirs of God, and joint-heirs with Christ; if so be that we suffer with him, that we may be also glorified together.[121]

That there are doctrinal differences between Spirit-filled Christians does create problems for the unity of the faith. Thus the Church has been given gifts of ministers by God for His Church:

> And he gave some, apostles; and some, prophets; and some, evangelists; and some, pastors and teachers; For the perfecting of the saints, for the work of the ministry, for the edifying of the body of Christ: Till we all come in the unity of the faith, and of the knowledge of the Son of God, unto a perfect man, unto the measure of the stature of the fulness of Christ: That we henceforth be no more children, tossed to and fro, and carried about with every wind of doctrine, by the sleight of men, and cunning craftiness, whereby they lie in wait to deceive; But speaking the truth in love, may grow up into him in all things, which is the head, even Christ: From whom the whole body fitly joined together and compacted by that which every joint supplieth, according to the effectual working in the measure of every part, maketh increase of the body unto the edifying of itself in love.[122]

Much of this thinking joins up the Cyrillic-Vincentian dimension of Catholicism with the Ignatian dimension and shows the essential unity of the different expressions of what it means to be Catholic. Tertullian expects there to be just one Christian Faith for his *reductio ad absurdum*[123] against Heretics to work:

> Grant, then, that all have erred; that the apostle was mistaken in giving his testimony; that the Holy Ghost had no such

---

[120] St Clement of Alexandria, Stromata VI. xv, Different Degrees of Knowledge (ANF II p 510-511)
[121] Romans viii.16-17
[122] Ephesians xii.11-16
[123] Notice that a *reductio ad absurdum* argument is a use of Reason about which Tertullian has expressed concerns.

> respect to any one (church) as to lead it into truth, although sent with this view by Christ, and for this asked of the Father that He might be the teacher of truth; grant, also, that He, the Steward of God, the Vicar of Christ, neglected His office, permitting the churches for a time to understand differently, (and) to believe differently, what He Himself was preaching by the apostles — is it likely that so many churches, and they so great, should have gone astray into one and the same faith? No casualty distributed among many men issues in one and the same result. Error of doctrine in the churches must necessarily have produced various issues. When, however, that which is deposited among many is found to be one and the same, it is not the result of error, but of tradition. Can any one, then, be reckless enough to say that they were in error who handed on the tradition?[124]

It is also to be remembered that Tertullian himself began a sect within the heretical Montanists[125] - a New Prophecy movement that claimed a new revelation superior to that of the Apostles.[126] It is the example of the Montanists who demonstrate what goes wrong when different spirits masquerade as the Holy Ghost. In this sense, both Spong and Schori also demonstrate elements of Montanist belief in that they challenge what the Church has always believed through a new prophecy.

St Jerome in AD385 speaks quite clearly against the New Prophetic movement known as Montanism:

> In the first place we differ from the Montanists regarding the rule of faith. We distinguish the Father, the Son, and the Holy Spirit as three persons, but unite them as one substance. They, on the other hand, following the doctrine of Sabellius, force the Trinity into the narrow limits of a single personality. We, while we do not encourage them, yet allow second marriages, since Paul bids the younger widows to marry.[127] They suppose a repetition of marriage a sin so awful that he who has committed it is to be regarded as an adulterer. We, according to the apostolic tradition (in which the whole world is at one with us), fast through one Lent yearly; whereas they keep three in the year as though three saviours had suffered. I do not mean, of course, that it is unlawful to fast at other times through the year — always excepting Pentecost — only that

---

[124] Tertullian, Prescription against Heretics xxviii (ANF III, p 256)
[125] (Quasten, 2000) II p 247
[126] (Damick, 2011) p 47
[127] I Timothy v.14

> while in Lent it is a duty of obligation, at other seasons it is a matter of choice. With us, again, the bishops occupy the place of the apostles, but with them a bishop ranks not first but third. For while they put first the patriarchs of Pepusa in Phrygia, and place next to these the ministers called stewards, the bishops are relegated to the third or almost the lowest rank. No doubt their object is to make their religion more pretentious by putting that last which we put first. Again they close the doors of the Church to almost every fault, while we read daily, *I desire the repentance of a sinner rather than his death,*[128] and *Shall they fall and not arise, says the Lord,*[129] and once more *Return ye backsliding children and I will heal your backslidings.*[130] Their strictness does not prevent them from themselves committing grave sins, far from it; but there is this difference between us and them, that, whereas they in their self-righteousness blush to confess their faults, we do penance for ours, and so more readily gain pardon for them.[131]

St Augustine also mentions that the "Tertullianists" – that is, a group of Montanists who followed Tertullian – had dwindled by the time of his episcopacy in Hippo:

> The Tertullianists take their name from Tertullian, whose many eloquent works are still read. Though steadily diminishing in numbers up to our time, they managed to survive to the last remnants in the city of Carthage. But when I found myself there several years ago, as I think you also remember, they disappeared completely. For the very few who were left passed into the Catholic Church and surrendered their basilica, which is even now a very famous one, to the Catholic Church.[132]

The major doctrinal blow against Montanism is given by the Second Oecumenical Council:

> But Eunomians, who are baptized with only one immersion, and Montanists, who are here called Phrygians, and Sabellians, who teach the identity of Father and Son, and do

---

[128] Ezekiel xviii.23
[129] Jeremiah viii.4
[130] Jeremiah iii.22
[131] St Jerome, Letter xli to Marcella (NPNF 2, VI, p55-56)
[132] St Augustine, On the Heresies lxxxvi, found in Migne's *Patrologia Latina*, XLII col 21-50. The English translation above comes from L.G.Muller, The "*De haeresibus of St. Augustine*" (Patristic Studies 90), Catholic University of America, Washington 1956.

> sundry other mischievous things, and [the partisans of] all other heresies— for there are many such here, particularly among those who come from the country of the Galatians:— all these, when they desire to turn to orthodoxy, we receive as heathen.[133]

While there is some debate as to whether this is a true canon of the Council, it exists in the Greek sources but not the Latin[134] and it is suggested that it forms part of a letter from the Church in Constantinople to Bishop Martyrus of Antioch. That it forms part of Canon XCV of the Council of Trullo gives it greater authority and shows that Montanism was certainly regarded as heretical sect earning widespread opprobrium.

The Holy Ghost is working for the unity: through Him we are converted to the truth of the Christian Faith and begin our journey back to Christ. Experience cannot be authoritative except in facilitating the individual's initial approach to the Church in which the Catholic Faith and practice may be found. However, by construction, the Catholic Faith contains everything that is necessary for anyone to find salvation in Jesus Christ. On the other hand, our experience of God, properly tested, is the motor that drives the Christian to deepen his faith in God and serve Him as best he can.

Anglican Catholicism and Cyrillic-Vincentian Catholicism

Having set out what is to be understood to be the Catholic Faith and the authorities by which doctrine is found to be consonant with the Faith or not, it is now necessary to understand how Anglican Catholicism sees itself in relationship with that Faith.

The ACC subscribes to the Affirmation of St Louis. This begins:

> We gather as people called by God to be faithful and obedient to Him. As the Royal Priestly People of God[135], the Church is called[136] to be, in fact, the manifestation of Christ in and to the world. True religion is revealed to man by God. We cannot decide what is truth, but rather (in obedience) ought to receive, accept, cherish, defend and teach what God has given us. The Church is created by God, and is beyond the ultimate control of man.[137]

---

[133] The first Oecumenical Council of Constantinople (AD381) "Canon VII" (NPNF2, XIV p 185),
[134] NPNF2, XIV p 184-5
[135] I Peter ii.9
[136] Hence the Church being called *ekklēsia* in Greek.
[137] Affirmation of St Louis, I.1

The Affirmation of St Louis may be seen to follow the above logic in demonstrating its adherence to the Catholic principles of Holy Scripture, Tradition and Reason. It subscribes to the movement of the soul towards God by the interpersonal revelation of the Holy Ghost as expressed by Craig and yet it recognises the call of the Spirit for the Unity of the Faith. If Christ is the Truth[138] then human beings are incompetent at discerning the truth apart from Christ and thus must be obedient to the revelation God has given to His Church.

> We repudiate all deviation or departure from the Faith, in whole or in part, and bear witness to these essential principles of evangelical Truth and apostolic Order[.][139]

As the ACC springs out from the Congress of St Louis and has the Affirmation as its founding document, the Church states clearly in its Canons how it intends to approach the question of Christian Doctrine:

> (a) The Constitution and Canons of The Anglican Catholic Church are based upon, necessarily frequently express, and must be consistent with, the beliefs of This Church. However, the positive law of This Church is not intended to, and does not, either formulate or create those beliefs but is, instead, subsidiary to and an outgrowth of them.
>
> (b) This Church adheres to the historic, distinctive Anglican approach to doctrinal and theological authority, which begins with Scripture as the inspired word of God containing all doctrines essential for salvation, as interpreted in the light of the Holy Tradition (which is, among other things, a summary of the Church's historic reflection upon the contents of Scripture), and, when necessary, the use of our God-given human reason in a manner consistent with the aforesaid Scripture and Tradition.
>
> (c) As set forth in The Solemn Declaration prefaced to The Constitution of This Church, and in The Affirmation of St. Louis, This Church claims, and has, no authority to contradict the central Traditions of the Church Catholic or to reach for

---

[138] St John xiv.6
[139] Affirmation of St Louis, I.1

itself conclusions that are not matters of the historic Catholic consensus.[140]

Thus, the intention to continue what the Catholic Faith is enshrined in how the ACC sees itself. The Affirmation of St Louis sets out clearly what it understands to be Christian Doctrine, namely as that contained in Scripture, Tradition and Creed.

Holy Scriptures

The Affirmation says quite clearly

> The Holy Scriptures of the Old and New Testaments as the authentic record of God's revelation of Himself, His saving activity, and moral demands - a revelation valid for all men and all time.[141]

While this largely speaks for itself, it is worth noting that the question remains about what constitutes Holy Scripture. The Protestant reformers left out of the canon of Scripture the books called Apocrypha, namely "the other Books (as Hierome saith) the Church doth read for example of life and instruction of manners; but yet doth it not apply them to establish any doctrine[.]"[142] Historically, the Church of England has included the Apocryphal books in the lectionary and a translation of them exists in the Authorised Version. The ACC says in its Constitution:

> The Authorised (King James) Version is the received Standard English translation of the Holy Scripture (Old Testament, New Testament, Apocrypha).[143]

Yet, with regard to the Scriptural authority of the Apocrypha there is some latitude following Article VI from the Church of England formularies. The acting-Primate of the ACC, the Most Rev Mark Haverland states:

> From this Article [i.e. Article VI] it is clear that Anglicans consider the Apocrypha to be part of the Bible and think that its stories are edifying and that its wisdom is instructive. However, Anglicans do not base doctrine…on the authority of the Apocrypha alone. Opinions vary about the Apocrypha in

---

[140] Anglican Catholic Church Canons, §2.2.01 Relationship between the Constitution and Canons and the Beliefs of This Church.
[141] The Affirmation of St Louis, I.2
[142] Article VI from the XXXIX Articles.
[143] Anglican Catholic Church Constitution, Article XIV, Section 4 (Of Translations of Holy Scripture)

> the Eastern Orthodox Church, but many reputable Orthodox theologians give it less authority than the Old or New Testament and would probably agree with this Anglican position.[144]

The Archbishop is alluding to the lack of consistency within the Church Fathers as to the level of authority that the Apocrypha possesses:

> Let not other books seduce your mind: for many malignant writings have been disseminated. The historical books are twelve in number by the Hebrew count, [then follow the names of the books of the Old Testament but Esther is omitted, one Esdras, and all the Deutero-Canonical books]. Thus there are twenty-two books of the Old Testament which correspond to the Hebrew letters. The number of the books of the New Mystery are Matthew, who wrote the Miracles of Christ for the Hebrews; Mark for Italy; Luke, for Greece; John, the enterer of heaven, was a preacher to all, then the Acts, the xiv. Epistles of Paul, the vii. Catholic Epistles, and so you have all the books. If there is any beside these, do not repute it genuine.[145]

And further, St Amphilochius demonstrates the same reticence about the Apocrypha's status in Holy Scripture:

> We should know that not every book which is called Scripture is to be received as a safe guide. For some are tolerably sound and others are more than doubtful. Therefore the books which the inspiration of God hath given I will enumerate. [Then follows a list of the proto-canonical books of the Old Testament, Esther alone being omitted. All the, deutero-canonical books are omitted. He then continues] to these some add Esther. I must now show what are the books of the New Testament. [Then follow all the books of the New Testament except the Revelation. He continues,] But some add to these the Revelation of John, but by far the majority say that it is spurious. This is the most true canon of the divinely given Scriptures.[146]

---

[144] (Haverland, 3rd Ed 2011) p 19
[145] From the Metre Poems of St. Gregory Theologus, Specifying which Books of the Old and New Testament Should Be Read. (NPNF2, XIV p 612)
[146] The Canon of St. Amphilochius on the Canon of Scripture, (NPNF2, XIV p 612)

In adhering to this rule, the ACC is found squarely in line with the historic Church of England, i.e. that of the time of the writing of the Articles.

The Creeds

On the position of the Creeds, the Affirmation says:

> The Nicene Creed as the authoritative summary of the chief articles of the Christian Faith, together with the Apostles' Creed, and that known as the Creed of St. Athanasius to be "thoroughly received and believed" in the sense they have had always in the Catholic Church.[147]

The Nicene Creed, or Nicene-Constantinopolitan Creed, stands at the centre of Christian Doctrine and has prime position over the Apostles' Creed and the "Athanasian" Creed which, although orthodox, are not products of an Oecumenical Council in the same manner as the Nicene Creed. That the ACC states its agreement with this puts it squarely in agreement with the Primitive Church and with the subsequent division into East and West.

Of course, the question of the *filioque* arises and it is vital that this be addressed as, first, it is a statement of belief in who God is, and second, how it came to be inserted in the Creed is a major source of contention. The Catholic Faith teaches that one person of the Trinity is called "Father", another "Son" and the third "Holy Ghost". Logic tells us that there cannot be a father without a child, nor a son without a father. So although the Father is God, and the Son is God, the Father cannot be a father were it not for the existence of the Son whom Christian doctrine shows is consubstantial with the Father, i.e. whatever the Father is, so is the Son. A created "Son" could not be worshipped as God for, in being created, "He" ceases to be God.

The Arian controversy came about from confusing the Greek idea of "cause" as a succession of events rather than an explanatory relationship. The substance of God is beyond the created Universe and thus this causal relationship between Father and Son is also beyond the imagination of the creature. By calling the Son "Eternally begotten", it is being stated categorically that the Father is causally responsible for the existence of the Son which is not representable in Time. This is a consequence of how the terms "father" and "son" are understood by man, and God Himself has used these very words when revealing Himself to His creation. Christianity proclaims its

---

[147] The Affirmation of St Louis, I.2

belief that God the Father is the Causeless Cause. If that is the case, then it follows that God is the eternal cause of the Holy Ghost too.

> The Holy Spirit Himself also, which operates in the prophets, we assert to be an effluence of God, flowing from Him, and returning back again like a beam of the sun.[148]

St Basil writes to his brother St Gregory of Nyssa concerning the relationship between the persons of the Holy Trinity.

> On the other hand there is a certain power subsisting without generation and without origination, which is the cause of the cause of all things. For the Son, by whom are all things, and with whom the Holy Ghost is inseparably conceived of, is of the Father. For it is not possible for any one to conceive of the Son if he be not previously enlightened by the Spirit. Since, then, the Holy Ghost, from Whom all the supply of good things for creation has its source, is attached to the Son, and with Him is inseparably apprehended, and has Its being attached to the Father, as cause, from Whom also It proceeds; It has this note of Its peculiar hypostatic nature, that It is known after the Son and together with the Son, and that It has Its subsistence of the Father. The Son, Who declares the Spirit proceeding from the Father through Himself and with Himself, shining forth alone and by only-begetting from the unbegotten light, so far as the peculiar notes are concerned, has nothing in common either with the Father or with the Holy Ghost. He alone is known by the stated signs. But God, Who is over all, alone has, as one special mark of His own hypostasis, His being Father, and His deriving His hypostasis from no cause; and through this mark He is peculiarly known. Wherefore in the communion of the substance we maintain that there is no mutual approach or intercommunion of those notes of indication perceived in the Trinity, whereby is set forth the proper peculiarity of the Persons delivered in the faith, each of these being distinctively apprehended by His own notes. Hence, in accordance with the stated signs of indication, discovery is made of the separation of the hypostases; while so far as relates to the infinite, the incomprehensible, the uncreate, the uncircumscribed, and similar attributes, there is no variableness in the life-giving nature; in that, I mean, of Father, Son, and Holy Ghost, but in

---

[148] Athenagoras of Athens (133-190), A Plea on behalf of Christians x (ANF II, p133)

> Them is seen a certain communion indissoluble and continuous.[149]

Another of the Cappadocian Fathers, St Gregory of Nazianzus (329 – 390) also speaks about this relationship, and makes mention of the idea of procession.

> The Father is Father, and is Unoriginate, for He is of no one; the Son is Son, and is not unoriginate, for He is of the Father. But if you take the word Origin in a temporal sense, He too is Unoriginate, for He is the Maker of Time, and is not subject to Time. The Holy Ghost is truly Spirit, coming forth from the Father indeed, but not after the manner of the Son, for it is not by Generation but by Procession (since I must coin a word for the sake of clearness); for neither did the Father cease to be Unbegotten because of His begetting something, nor the Son to be begotten because He is of the Unbegotten (how could that be?), nor is the Spirit changed into Father or Son because He proceeds, or because He is God— though the ungodly do not believe it.[150]

The word "procession" that St Gregory uses is the same that is found in St John's Gospel in Our Lord's final sermon to His disciples at the Last Supper.

> But when the Comforter is come, whom I will send unto you from the Father, even the Spirit of truth, which proceedeth (ἐκπορεύεται - *ekporeuetai*) from the Father, he shall testify of me:[151]

The same word is used to denote the idea of emerging from something else. In St Luke's Gospel, that word is used in the description of how people react to the Lord's teaching:

> And all bare him witness, and wondered at the gracious words which proceeded (ἐκπορευομένοις - *ekporeuomenois*) out of his mouth. And they said, Is not this Joseph's son?[152]

The Holy Spirit is God and there is a clear causal relationship between Father and Spirit that is not the same as Father and Son. The Holy Ghost seems to emerge from

---

[149] St Basil, Epistle XXXVIII.iv (NPNF2, VI p138-139)
[150] St Gregory of Nazianzus, Oration XXXIX, On the Holy Lights xii (NPNF2. VII p356)
[151] St John xv.26
[152] St Luke iv.22

the Father as one might emerge from a city, or as a word may emerge from the mind. These are analogies though and their limitations as analogies must be noted.

The Spirit, however, is certainly sent forth by the Son just as willingly as the Son accepts His Incarnation. Our Lord Jesus in John xx.22 breathes on His disciples and tells them to receive the Holy Spirit. This has definitely influenced St Augustine:

> Why, then, should we not believe that the Holy Spirit proceedeth also from the Son, seeing that He is likewise the Spirit of the Son? For did He not so proceed, He could not, when showing Himself to His disciples after the resurrection, have breathed upon them, and said, "Receive the Holy Spirit." For what else was signified by such a breathing upon them, but that from Him also the Holy Spirit proceedeth?[153]

Our Lord also says,

> Nevertheless I tell you the truth; It is expedient for you that I go away: for if I go not away, the Comforter will not come unto you; but if I depart, I will send (πέμψω) him unto you.[154]

Holy Scripture is clear that there is some relationship between the Holy Ghost and the Son. St Paul twice makes this connection:

> And because ye are sons, God hath sent forth the Spirit of his Son into your hearts, crying, Abba, Father.[155]

> But ye are not in the flesh, but in the Spirit, if so be that the Spirit of God dwell in you. Now if any man have not the Spirit of Christ, he is none of his.[156]

It might be said that Our Lord is indeed involved in the mission of the Holy Ghost in time, but is not the Eternal Cause which can only be the Father, yet it is also to be noted that the ministration of the Holy Ghost does operate with mankind before the Incarnation.[157] Nevertheless, in being breathed upon after the Resurrection, the Apostles are empowered to set about gathering the Church of God. Human beings therefore experience the Holy Ghost only on account of the involvement of the Son. This is one way of reading St Augustine's ideas in conjunction with the Eastern

---

[153] St Augustine of Hippo, Tractates on the Gospel of St John, xcix.7 (NPNF1, VII p 383)
[154] St John xvi.7
[155] Galatians iv.6
[156] Romans viii.9
[157] E.g. Exodus xxxv.31, Numbers xxiv.2, and I Samuel x.10

Orthodox Faith. St Basil and other Church Fathers would be happy to speak of the cause of the Holy Ghost as being from the Father through the Son. Indeed this is what St Maximus the Confessor (580-662) tried to put forward.

> The Church of God, worthy of all praise, is a lampstand wholly of gold, pure and without stain, undefiled and without blemish, receptacle of the true light that never dims… The lamp above her is the true light of the Father which lights up every man coming into this world, Our Lord Jesus Christ, became light and called such… And if Christ is the head of the Church according to human understanding, then he is the one who by his nature has the Spirit and has bestowed the charisms of the Spirit on the Church… For the Holy Spirit, just as he belongs to the nature of God the Father according to his essence so he also belongs to the nature of the Son according to his essence, since he proceeds inexpressibly from the Father through his begotten Son and bestows on the lampstand – the Church – his energies as through a lantern.[158]

St Maximus is echoing an older idea that perhaps is first met in Tertullian:

> But as for me, who derive the Son from no other source but from the substance of the Father, and (represent Him) as doing nothing without the Father's will, and as having received all power from the Father, how can I be possibly destroying the Monarchy from the faith, when I preserve it in the Son just as it was committed to Him by the Father? The same remark (I wish also to be formally) made by me with respect to the third degree in the Godhead, because I believe the Spirit to proceed from no other source than from the Father through the Son.[159]

And it would seem that this is how he would interpret *ex Patre Filioque procedit*:

> I should not hesitate, indeed, to call the tree the son or offspring of the root, and the river of the fountain, and the ray of the sun; because every original source is a parent, and everything which issues from the origin is an offspring. Much more is (this true of) the Word of God, who has actually received as His own peculiar designation the name of Son. But still the tree is not severed from the root, nor the river from the fountain, nor the ray from the sun; nor, indeed, is the

---

[158] St Maximus the Confessor, *Quaestiones ad Thalassium* lxiii in (Siecienski, 2012) p 77
[159] Tertullian, Against Praxeas iv (ANF III, p 599)

> Word separated from God. Following, therefore, the form of these analogies, I confess that I call God and His Word— the Father and His Son— two. For the root and the tree are distinctly two things, but correlatively joined; the fountain and the river are also two forms, but indivisible; so likewise the sun and the ray are two forms, but coherent ones. Everything which proceeds from something else must needs be second to that from which it proceeds, without being on that account separated. Where, however, there is a second, there must be two; and where there is a third, there must be three. Now the Spirit indeed is third from God and the Son; just as the fruit of the tree is third from the root, or as the stream out of the river is third from the fountain, or as the apex of the ray is third from the sun. Nothing, however, is alien from that original source whence it derives its own properties. In like manner the Trinity, flowing down from the Father through intertwined and connected steps, does not at all disturb the Monarchy, while it at the same time guards the state of the Economy.[160]

Origen (185 – 254) also develops Tertullian's ideas on the relationship between the hypostases of the Trinity:

> We consider, therefore, that there are three hypostases, the Father and the Son and the Holy Spirit; and at the same time we believe nothing to be uncreated but the Father. We therefore, as the more pious and the truer course, admit that all things were made by the Logos, and that the Holy Spirit is the most excellent and the first in order of all that was made by the Father through Christ. And this, perhaps, is the reason why the Spirit is not said to be God's own Son. The Only-begotten only is by nature and from the beginning a Son, and the Holy Spirit seems to have need of the Son, to minister to Him His essence, so as to enable Him not only to exist, but to be wise and reasonable and just, and all that we must think of Him as being. All this He has by participation of the character of Christ, of which we have spoken above.[161]

This means that there is only one causal procession, not a double causal procession. It is a procession from the Father-and-the-Son – a single procession – not a procession from the Father and a separate procession from the Son – i.e. a double

---
[160] Tertullian, Against Praxeas viii (ANF III, p 602)
[161] Origen, Commentary on St John's Gospel, II.vi (ANF IX, p328-329)

procession. Even then, as St Maximus says, how this causal procession works is not available to earthly thought.

However this causation works, St Basil makes an admonition:

> Do you maintain that the Son is numbered under the Father, and the Spirit under the Son, or do you confine your sub-numeration to the Spirit alone? If, on the other hand, you apply this sub-numeration also to the Son, you revive what is the same impious doctrine, the unlikeness of the substance, the lowliness of rank, the coming into being in later time, and once for all, by this one term, you will plainly again set circling all the blasphemies against the Only-begotten. To controvert these blasphemies would be a longer task than my present purpose admits of; and I am the less bound to undertake it because the impiety has been refuted elsewhere to the best of my ability. If on the other hand they suppose the sub-numeration to benefit the Spirit alone, they must be taught that the Spirit is spoken of together with the Lord in precisely the same manner in which the Son is spoken of with the Father. The name of the Father and of the Son and of the Holy Ghost is delivered in like manner, and, according to the co-ordination of words delivered in baptism, the relation of the Spirit to the Son is the same as that of the Son to the Father. And if the Spirit is co-ordinate with the Son, and the Son with the Father, it is obvious that the Spirit is also co-ordinate with the Father. When then the names are ranked in one and the same co-ordinate series, what room is there for speaking on the one hand of connumeration, and on the other of sub-numeration?[162]

In all reasoning there must be a painful awareness of the limitations of human apprehension of true divinity. The only things that can be said about God are pale shadows[163] concepts of the truth, concepts which Christians are able to formulate or articulate between themselves but lack the dimensions that only the Beatific Vision can supply.

The second problem concerns the insertion of the *filioque* in the Creed. The Canons of the Council of Ephesus were written at a time when Nestorius was trying to force through changes to the Christian Faith.

---

[162] St Basil, On the Holy Spirit xvii (NPNF2, VIII p 27)
[163] I Corinthians xiii.8-13

When these things had been read, the holy Synod decreed that it is unlawful for any man to bring forward, or to write, or to compose a different Faith as a rival to that established by the holy Fathers assembled with the Holy Ghost in Nicaea.

> But those who shall dare to compose a different faith, or to introduce or offer it to persons desiring to turn to the acknowledgment of the truth, whether from Heathenism or from Judaism, or from any heresy whatsoever, shall be deposed, if they be bishops or clergymen; bishops from the episcopate and clergymen from the clergy; and if they be laymen, they shall be anathematized.

> And in like manner, if any, whether bishops, clergymen, or laymen, should be discovered to hold or teach the doctrines contained in the Exposition introduced by the Presbyter Charisius concerning the Incarnation of the Only-Begotten Son of God, or the abominable and profane doctrines of Nestorius, which are subjoined, they shall be subjected to the sentence of this holy and ecumenical Synod. So that, if it be a bishop, he shall be removed from his bishopric and degraded; if it be a clergyman, he shall likewise be stricken from the clergy; and if it be a layman, he shall be anathematized, as has been afore said.[164]

Also at the Council of Chalcedon, we also find:

> These things, therefore, having been expressed by us with the greatest accuracy and attention, the holy Ecumenical Synod defines that no one shall be suffered to bring forward a different faith, nor to write, nor to put together, nor to excogitate, nor to teach it to others. But such as dare either to put together another faith, or to bring forward or to teach or to deliver a different Creed to as wish to be converted to the knowledge of the truth, from the Gentiles, or Jews or any heresy whatever, if they be Bishops or clerics let them be deposed, the Bishops from the Episcopate, and the clerics from the clergy; but if they be monks or laics: let them be anathematized.[165]

The *filioque* was probably first inserted into the Creed at Toledo in 587, though there is a possibility that it was inserted in the Creed at the Council of Selucia-Ctesiphon

---

[164] Council of Ephesus, Canon VII (NPNF2, XIV, p 231)
[165] Council of Chalcedon, Fifth Session (NPNF 2, XIV, p 265)

in 410. The problem is that it violates the canons of the Council of Ephesus and Chalcedon because it does make the Creed substantially different. While arguments about it raged through the sixth to eleventh centuries (such as the Schism of Photius in the ninth century), it was in 1014 that Pope Benedict VIII had it included in the Creed at Mass for political purposes, and thus sealed the Schism which was nominally put into effect in 1054.[166]

Thus, the issue is whether a Pope can override the Canons of an Oecumenical Council especially at the behest of a secular ruler – in this case King Henry II of Germany. The Eastern Orthodox believe that he cannot: Anglican Catholics agree with them.

Why, then, should the *filioque* matter? Why should space be devoted to it? The *filioque* clause is an exemplar of the divisions within the Catholic Church and brings to the foreground the decisions that modern Catholics have to make and which will colour their relationships with others. It is the Anglican Catholic view that the *filioque* is not meant to be in the Creed. Anglican Catholic Archbishop Mark Haverland puts the position forward thus:

> The *filioque* should not remain in the authorised text of the Creed, because it was added unlawfully, is patient of misinterpretation, and is a grave obstacle to reunion between Eastern Orthodox and Anglican Catholics.[167]

As might be expected, effecting the change to remove the *filioque* from the Book of Common Prayer is a complicated synodal process which involves consultation in the Church at every level. Given that the ACC is relatively new as an organisation, the synodic process cannot begin and, until it does, Anglican Catholics are faced with a choice:

- keep it in the Book of Common Prayer but omit it when reciting the Creed;
- keep it in the Book of Common Prayer but understand it as "from the Father *through* the Son" following the examples of St Maximos and Tertullian.

Tradition

On the question of the authority of Tradition, the Affirmation says:

---

[166] See (Siecienski, 2012)
[167] (Haverland, 3rd Ed 2011) p 143

> The received Tradition of the Church and its teachings as set forth by "the ancient catholic bishops and doctors," and especially as defined by the Seven Ecumenical Councils of the undivided Church, to the exclusion of all errors, ancient and modern.[168]

In addition to this, the Affirmation makes a very clear statement about Catholic Authority:

> We acknowledge that rule of faith laid down by St. Vincent of Lerins: "Let us hold that which has been believed everywhere, always and by all, for that is truly and properly Catholic."[169]

This demonstrates that, from the point of view of intellectual assent, the ACC is properly Catholic in the Cyrillic-Vincentian sense. Further, the Canons of the ACC make it clear what it considers to be doctrinal and canonical:

> This Church submits itself and subscribes to the Seven Holy Oecumenical Councils of the undivided Primitive Catholic Church and their Doctrine, Definitions, Letters, Epistles, Acts, and Decrees, both doctrinal and synodal, and the Letters and Decrees of the Regional Councils or Synods and of the Fathers received, accepted, and affirmed by the same Oecumenical Councils, all as received in the Church of England through the year 1543, as well as the Canons, Canonical Acts and Decrees, and the Rulings Canonical thereof or made therein, and the Canonical principles expressed therein, as have been accustomed and used in the Church since their adoption and which have neither been expressly altered or amended by positive action of this Church nor have fallen into and remained in desuetude...

There then follows a list of these Canons, Canonical Acts and Decrees which are mentioned and referenced by the Seven Oecumenical Councils and thus cements the doctrine of the ACC in place with the Orthodox Church.

Conclusion

Starting from the historical facts of the Life, Death and Resurrection of Our Lord Jesus Christ, it has been shown that the truth that the Church has received is revealed in Holy Scripture, in Holy Tradition and in Right Reasoning therefrom and

---

[168] The Affirmation of St Louis, I.2
[169] Affirmation of St Louis, end of the Preface.

that these fit together as an indivisible whole rather than three separable strands. It has been shown that there has been a Church which has held to these principles and, in holding these principles, can be described as Catholic in the sense meant by St Cyril of Jerusalem in his Catechetical Lectures and in the sense of St Vincent of Lerins. It has been shown that since the separation between the Eastern and Western Churches, no further Oecumenical development can take place and that no further doctrine can be accepted as properly Catholic until there is a formal Council of the reunited Church. Further, it has been shown that the Church believes that the Holy Ghost is directly responsible for presenting the individual with the truth at the subjective level which is then demonstrated objectively in the individual's subsequent declaration of faith and active assent to the doctrine of the Catholic Church.

It has been shown that Anglican Catholics hold to this understanding of ecclesial authority in their foundational documents and have some claim to be considered Catholic in the Cyrillic-Vincentian sense. Faith is not an intellectual or philosophical exercise and requires instantiation and *conversatio mores*. Thus for this understanding of Catholicism to have any grounding in practice, it is necessary to show that the ACC is Catholic in the Ignatian sense.

Ignatian Catholicism and the ACC

The Catholic point of view on history, then, comes from living the faith, not by indifferent and arbitrary academic study.[170] The Catholic Faith is in Christians' blood, in their heritage and in their way of thinking. The Church is the Body of Christ and therefore has a visible, organic unity across Time and Space since Christ is the "same yesterday, and to day, and for ever." In many respects, the Church is like the family of Abraham which, under Jacob, formed one family in twelve tribes formed with the sons of Jacob. This can be seen from Our Lord's description of Himself as the true vine:

> I am the true vine, and my Father is the husbandman. Every branch in me that beareth not fruit he taketh away: and every branch that beareth fruit, he purgeth it, that it may bring forth more fruit. Now ye are clean through the word which I have spoken unto you. Abide in me, and I in you. As the branch cannot bear fruit of itself, except it abide in the vine; no more can ye, except ye abide in me. I am the vine, ye are the branches: He that abideth in me, and I in him, the same bringeth forth much fruit: for without me ye can do nothing. If a man abide not in me, he is cast forth as a branch, and is withered; and men gather them, and cast them into the fire, and they are burned. If ye abide in me, and my words abide in you, ye shall ask what ye will, and it shall be done unto you. Herein is my Father glorified, that ye bear much fruit; so shall ye be my disciples. As the Father hath loved me, so have I loved you: continue ye in my love. If ye keep my commandments, ye shall abide in my love; even as I have kept my Father's commandments, and abide in his love.[171]

St Paul uses the analogy of Israel as the vine to explain Our Lord's words further:

> For I speak to you Gentiles, inasmuch as I am the apostle of the Gentiles, I magnify mine office: If by any means I may provoke to emulation them which are my flesh, and might save some of them. For if the casting away of them be the reconciling of the world, what shall the receiving of them be,

---

[170] C.f. I Corinthians viii.1-3. One may lord one's superior knowledge of things over another but the way of love (I Corinthians xiii) demands an active care for one another.
[171] St John xv.1-10

> but life from the dead? For if the firstfruit be holy, the lump is also holy: and if the root be holy, so are the branches. And if some of the branches be broken off, and thou, being a wild olive tree, wert graffed in among them, and with them partakest of the root and fatness of the olive tree; Boast not against the branches. But if thou boast, thou bearest not the root, but the root thee. Thou wilt say then, The branches were broken off, that I might be graffed in. Well; because of unbelief they were broken off, and thou standest by faith. Be not highminded, but fear: For if God spared not the natural branches, take heed lest he also spare not thee.[172]

Christians have the same parentage in the Catholic Faith but their own cultural expression of it. This is made clear from the decision about how the Jews and the Gentiles are to be Christians together. The decree from the first Council of Jerusalem headed by St James decides not to force Jews to become Gentiles nor *vice versa* but rather that there should be common regard for the worship of God.

> It seemed good unto us, being assembled with one accord, to send chosen men unto you with our beloved Barnabas and Paul, Men that have hazarded their lives for the name of our Lord Jesus Christ. We have sent therefore Judas and Silas, who shall also tell you the same things by mouth. For it seemed good to the Holy Ghost, and to us, to lay upon you no greater burden than these necessary things; That ye abstain from meats offered to idols, and from blood, and from things strangled, and from fornication: from which if ye keep yourselves, ye shall do well. Fare ye well.[173]

Thus Gentiles are not required to observe Jewish customs, nor are they bound by the laws of kosher. These expressions of Jewish worship are not incorporated into the Gentile culture: it is necessary to be bound to the worship of God (i.e. refraining from idolatry) and obey His moral standards (i.e. refraining from fornication). This demonstrates that Christianity legitimately possesses cultural expressions of worship. The consequence is that there are a proliferation of "local" rites and customs of worship based upon the same Catholic Faith – a fact that will become important in examining the Anglican nature of the Church of England and the ACC. If there is to be any cultural element to the expression of Christian worship, then there needs to be an expression of the Catholic Faith – an expression which St Ignatius has mentioned above.

---

[172] Romans xi.13-21
[173] Acts xv.25-28

Orthokoinōnia

As has been seen above, St Ignatius says:

> Wherever the bishop shall appear, there let the multitude [of the people] also be; even as, wherever Jesus Christ is, there is the Catholic Church.

The key idea is that local expressions of the Church should be in communion and this is the central unifying principle behind the practice.

The meaning of Communion

The word "communion" is used thrice in the Authorised Version of the Bible and all occurrences occur in both of St Paul's letters to the Corinthians.

> The cup of blessing which we bless, is it not the communion of the blood of Christ? The bread which we break, is it not the communion of the body of Christ?[174]

> Be ye not unequally yoked together with unbelievers: for what fellowship hath righteousness with unrighteousness? and what communion hath light with darkness?[175]

> The grace of the Lord Jesus Christ, and the love of God, and the communion of the Holy Ghost, be with you all. Amen.[176]

The word "communion" is used to translate the Greek word κοινωνία – *koinōnia* – which conveys commonality, associateship, affinity or fellowship. That sense of the word may be seen used in respect of gatherings of the Church around the Apostles and the teaching that they have received from God,[177] of communicating with other Christians,[178] or even charitable donation.[179] The sense is quite clear that *koinōnia* involves some reaching out to others as an expression of community.

This is presented most clearly in the sense of celebrating the Eucharist together. As I Corinthians x.16 shows us, the height of this communion is that Catholics all share

---

[174] I Corinthians x.16,
[175] II Corinthians vi.14
[176] II Corinthians xiii.14
[177] E.g. Acts ii.42, II Corinthians viii.4, Philippians i.5, Philippians ii.1, I John i.6
[178] E.g. Philemon 6, Hebrews xiii.16
[179] E.g. Romans xv.26, II Corinthians xi.13

in the communion of the Body and Blood of Christ. The Holy Mass, then, is a meeting ground in which Catholics have this fellowship with each other and with Christ.

> For we being many are one bread, and one body: for we are all partakers of that one bread.[180]

Of course, not every Christian believes the same thing about the Eucharist. The ACC believes that there is a form of transubstantiation which is neither as technical nor as reliant on Aristotelian metaphysics as that understood by the Roman Catholic Church. The Roman Catholic Church denies communion to those whom it believes have rejected the Catholic priesthood or their doctrine of the Eucharist.

> Ecclesial communities derived from the Reformation and separated from the Catholic Church, "have not preserved the proper reality of the Eucharistic mystery in its fullness, especially because of the absence of the sacrament of Holy Orders." It is for this reason that Eucharistic intercommunion with these communities is not possible for the Catholic Church. However these ecclesial communities, "when they commemorate the Lord's death and resurrection in the Holy Supper . . . profess that it signifies life in communion with Christ and await his coming in glory."[181]

Here arises a definition of what it means to be in communion. Two ecclesial bodies are in communion if each body recognises that the other truly celebrates the Mass and consecrates the Body and Blood of Christ. If Christ is truly present at the Masses of Church A and Church B, then Church A and Church B are both in communion with Christ and therefore with one another. If Church A does not believe that Church B truly makes really present the Body and Blood of Christ then they are not in communion – at least in Church A's eyes.

If Church A recognises that Church B truly celebrates the Mass then there must be some recognition by Church A that the sacramental ministers of Church B possess the same authority and grace in order to effect the sacrament as in Church A. In so doing, there is good reason for Church A to believe that Church B has a valid priesthood and that, at least at the level of the Mass, the two ministers are interchangeable. Further, this must also imply that the means of making ministers of the Eucharist in Church B is valid in Church A's eyes. Thus, at the level of making ministers of the Eucharist, the ministers of ordination of Church A must be interchangeable with those of B. From this, it may be seen that the recognition of

---

[180] I Corinthians x.17
[181] (Vatican, 2002) ¶1400

communion between two churches leads to an admission that there is a functional interchangeability of clergy. A formal declaration of *communicatio in sacris* between two bodies would need to be worked out at the level of the two canonical structures. This has been very much the basis of the drive for organic unity between Continuing Anglican bodies.

There is a further point to make which becomes important when discussing the origins of the Continuing Anglican Movement. Suppose that, within Church B there is a subset S of ministers which Church B recognises as true ministers of the Eucharist but Church A does not. Clearly, Church B regards ministers within S to be interchangeable with those who are not. Church A, however, does not. It becomes a point of logic[182] to show that Church A does not believe that Church B effects a true Eucharist. This does call into question whether a communion can be truly impaired rather than completely fractured. For example, the Church of England possesses this logical tension with the Forward in Faith Movement claiming an impairment of communion with the rest of the Anglican Communion which accepts the ordination of women.

This question of being in communion brings up the notion of *orthokoinōnia* i.e. that there is a right way of being in communion with the bishop and with Christians around the world and that is the discernment of the body of Christ in the Eucharist. While this question is addressed below, there is still the question of how far being in communion extends. Certainly, it is world-wide but can it be time-wide?

The Communion of the Saints

The Apostles' Creed states the Christian's belief in the Communion of the Saints, and this colours the understanding of human relationships by including those who have gone before. The letter to the Hebrews states:

> Let us hold fast the profession of our faith without wavering; (for he is faithful that promised;) And let us consider one another to provoke unto love and to good works: Not forsaking

---

[182] It has been established that:

(A recognises the Eucharist of B) ⇒ (A believes that the ministers of B are interchangeable with those of A).

The contrapositive of this is:

(A does not believe that the ministers of B are interchangeable with those of A) ⇒ (A does not recognise the Eucharist of B).

> the assembling of ourselves together, as the manner of some
> is; but exhorting one another: and so much the more, as ye see
> the day approaching.[183]

In Acts, it can be seen that "all that believed were together, and had all things common."[184] Further, St Paul talks clearly of the essential unity of the Body of Christ:

> For as we have many members in one body, and all members
> have not the same office: So we, being many, are one body in
> Christ, and every one members one of another.[185]

If this is true, and individuals are to see themselves as essentially united to each other in love, then does this unity end at death? Given the many references to the resurrection of the dead, the cloud of witnesses in Hebrews xii, and the multitudes of saints in the Revelation of St John, it is hard to see how this unity could be otherwise. If human beings are united to Christ and Christ is alive then we are united with those Christians who have, like St Stephen, "fallen asleep".[186]

St John Chrysostom (349-407) says of this, "Consider what an advance was here immediately! For the fellowship was not only in prayers, nor in doctrine alone, but also in (πολιτεία) social relations."[187] The use of "Our Father" in the Lord's Prayer is a deliberate and direct teaching from Our Lord Jesus Christ. It shows very carefully that God is the father of every human being and that thus all are related as family to each other. His command to love each other as oneself clearly shows that no-one can see himself as separate from any other.

This is particularly true of the Church. Human beings are all united in Christ. St Paul says to the Galatians:

> There is neither Jew nor Greek, there is neither bond nor free,
> there is neither male nor female: for ye are all one in Christ
> Jesus.[188]

..."for", as St Ignatius of Antioch says, "there is one nature, and one family of mankind."[189]

---

[183] Hebrews x.23-25
[184] Acts ii.44
[185] Romans xii.4-5
[186] Acts vii.60
[187] St John Chrysostom, Homily vii on the Acts of the Apostles (NPNF XI, p45)
[188] Galatians iii.28
[189] St Ignatius of Antioch Epistle to the Philadelphians iv. (ANF I, p81)

Our Lord states that, "there is joy in the presence of the angels of God over one sinner that repenteth."[190] This shows the solidarity that those in Heaven have with us on earth. The Communion of Saints is a real and Catholic Doctrine and means that all Christians have complete solidarity with those who have gone before. They are still part of the Church.

Such a solidarity to be faithful to other Christians disallows the fact that one just happens to be alive in time now to hold an authority over the Church of the present age. This is something that many modern Christians often forget: the individual might be alive now in time, but that same individual also possesses the opportunity to be alive in eternity with God. Eternal life trumps temporal and temporary life by reason of being united with God. Sometimes, modern Christians act as if this life is all there is, even if they believe otherwise.

The main and highly important conclusion that can be drawn from the existence of the Communion of the Saints is that the notion of History for an Anglican Catholic is not something that can be studied dispassionately by dissecting "Then" from "Now". Those alive now are that part of Christian History which just happens to be "Now" and will soon pass into "Then". Thus those alive at a particular time cannot not speak for the whole of time: to argue that the circumstances that surround the Church at a given time have the authority to alter the Church's teaching received from the beginning is like a leaf trying to dictate to the whole plant where it should stand in the garden. Pope St John Paul II said in his visit to Scotland in 1982:

> as believers, we are constantly exposed to pressures by modern society which would compel us to conform to the standards of this secular age, substitute new proprieties, restrict our aspirations at risk of compromising our Christian conscience.[191]

This gives weight to G. K. Chesterton's famous comment about the Democracy of the Dead and demonstrates clearly that the Vincentian-Cyrillic Catholicism is merely a restatement of Ignatian Catholicism since every Christian holds to the same Faith and receives the same sacraments from the same priesthood at the re-presentation of the same single atoning sacrifice. Alterations to the Faith, especially to the sacraments and morals, separate human beings in Time and breach this Communion. Such breaches have severe repercussions for those who are yet to

---

[190] St Luke xv.10
[191] https://www.dailyrecord.co.uk/news/uk-world-news/the-first-visit-looking-back-at-pope-1069954 (Accessed 23rd March 2021)

come. The Jewish People have this sense of tending to the future generations which Christians have inherited through them:

> Hear my law, O my people: incline your ears unto the words of my mouth.
>
> I will open my mouth in a parable: I will declare hard sentences of old;
>
> Which we have heard and known: and such as our fathers have told us;
>
> That we should not hide them from the children of the generations to come: but to shew the honour of the Lord, his mighty and wonderful works that he hath done.[192]

Likewise, St Paul urges the celebration of Holy Communion and the reification of *anamnesis* is to be handed on faithfully.[193]

This understanding has been enshrined within The Affirmation of St Louis which declares:

> Incompetence of Church Bodies to Alter Truth
> We disclaim any right or competence to suppress, alter or amend any of the ancient Ecumenical Creeds and definitions of Faith, to set aside or depart from Holy Scripture, or to alter or deviate from the essential prerequisites of any Sacrament.

The Body and Blood of Christ

The centrality of the nature of the Eucharist, then, is vital in understanding the nature of what it means to be in communion. This is not just a gathering of like-minded individuals at prayer. St Paul's words in I Corinthians x.16 make it quite clear that it is a communion of the Body and Blood of Christ. While prayer meetings are true and godly activities St Paul has something more objective and yet something fundamentally intimate in mind about the relationship between Man and God.

---

[192] Psalm lxxviii.1-4
[193] I Corinthians xi.23

The Real Presence

First, there is the question as to how communion is achieved through the Eucharist. Our Lord says, "For my flesh is meat indeed, and my blood is drink indeed."[194] This little word "indeed" (*vero* in Latin, ἀληθῶς in Greek) is significant: it means nothing less than truth: Jesus' flesh is really meat; Jesus' blood is really drink. Followers of Christ are to eat and drink the Body and Blood of Christ and this is why it scandalises so many disciples in John vi. The Church Fathers are fairly conclusive on this point.

St Ignatius of Antioch testifies

> I desire the bread of God, the heavenly bread, the bread of life, which is the flesh of Jesus Christ, the Son of God, who became afterwards of the seed of David and Abraham; and I desire the drink of God, namely His blood, which is incorruptible love and eternal life.[195]

St Justin Martyr agrees:

> And this food is called among us Εὐχαριστία, of which no one is allowed to partake but the man who believes that the things which we teach are true, and who has been washed with the washing that is for the remission of sins, and unto regeneration, and who is so living as Christ has enjoined. For not as common bread and common drink do we receive these; but in like manner as Jesus Christ our Saviour, having been made flesh by the Word of God, had both flesh and blood for our salvation, so likewise have we been taught that the food which is blessed by the prayer of His word, and from which our blood and flesh by transmutation are nourished, is the flesh and blood of that Jesus who was made flesh. For the apostles, in the memoirs composed by them, which are called Gospels, have thus delivered unto us what was enjoined upon them; that Jesus took bread, and when He had given thanks, said, This do in remembrance of Me,[196] this is My body; and that, after the same manner, having taken the cup and given thanks, He said, This is My blood; and gave it to them alone. Which the wicked devils have imitated in the mysteries of Mithras, commanding the same thing to be done. For, that bread and a cup of water are placed with certain incantations

---

[194] St John vi.55
[195] St Ignatius, Epistle to the Romans vii. (ANF, I, p76)
[196] St Luke xxii.19

in the mystic rites of one who is being initiated, you either know or can learn.[197]

As does St Irenaeus:

> But how can they be consistent with themselves, [when they say] that the bread over which thanks have been given is the body of their Lord, and the cup His blood, if they do not call Himself the Son of the Creator of the world, that is, His Word, through whom the wood fructifies, and the fountains gush forth, and the earth gives first the blade, then the ear, then the full grain in the ear?[198]
>
> Then, again, how can they say that the flesh, which is nourished with the body of the Lord and with His blood, goes to corruption, and does not partake of life? Let them, therefore, either alter their opinion, or cease from offering the things just mentioned. But our opinion is in accordance with the Eucharist, and the Eucharist in turn establishes our opinion. For we offer to Him His own, announcing consistently the fellowship and union of the flesh and Spirit. For as the bread, which is produced from the earth, when it receives the invocation of God, is no longer common bread, but the Eucharist, consisting of two realities, earthly and heavenly; so also our bodies, when they receive the Eucharist, are no longer corruptible, having the hope of the resurrection to eternity.[199]

Finally, St Cyril says:

> Then having sanctified ourselves by these spiritual Hymns, we beseech the merciful God to send forth His Holy Spirit upon the gifts lying before Him; that He may make the Bread the Body of Christ, and the Wine the Blood of Christ; for whatsoever the Holy Ghost has touched, is surely sanctified and changed.[200]

And this is affirmed also by the tomb of Abercius, Tertullian, St Hippolytus, St Clement of Alexandria, Origen, St Ephraim the Syrian, St Hilary of Poitiers, St Gregory of Nyssa, Theodore of Mopsuestia, St John Chrysostom, St Ambrose, St

---

[197] St Justin Martyr, First Apology lxvi (ANF, I, p185)
[198] St Mark iv.28
[199] St Irenaeus of Lyons, Against Heresies IV,xviii.4-5 (ANF, I, p486)
[200] St Cyril of Jerusalem, Catechetical Lectures xxiii.7 (NPNF2, VII, p154)

Augustine, and others. This really does rule out what has since become known as Zwinglism where the bread and wine are merely symbolic, and Receptionism in which the actions of eating and drinking the elements become the actions of eating the Body and Blood of Christ.

Consecration does indeed effect a real change in the bread and wine. Anglican Catholics are therefore bound to believe the consecrated elements at Mass are the real Body and Blood of Christ. How else can incorruptibility be put on as St Paul urges in I Corinthians xv.53-54?

The Sacrifice of the Mass

The second aspect of Communion is that of atonement, i.e. returning to fellowship and being at one with God, and the rôle that the consecration of the Body and Blood of Christ plays in this. In the Old Testament, i.e. the Old Covenant, this involves the notion of sacrifice and consequently the New Testament describes how that sacrificial system of the Jewish people is to be understood by Christians as a prefiguration of the sacrifice of Christ.

The first step is to look at the historical context of the first Mass. Any reading of the Torah shows very clearly that there was a system of sacrifices set up by God in order for the people of Israel to deepen their covenantal relationship with God. Yet it is clear that these are largely a temporary system before one better arrives. The prophet Malachi predicts the end of this system of Jewish sacrifice:

> Who is there even among you that would shut the doors for nought? neither do ye kindle fire on mine altar for nought. I have no pleasure in you, saith the LORD of hosts, neither will I accept an offering at your hand. For from the rising of the sun even unto the going down of the same my name shall be great among the Gentiles; and in every place incense shall be offered unto my name, and a pure offering: for my name shall be great among the heathen, saith the LORD of hosts.[201]

The timing of the Last Supper is crucial: according to the Gospels[202] it occurs at the time of the great Jewish sacrifice of Passover and immediately before the

---

[201] Malachi i.10-11
[202] The Synoptic Gospels (St Matthew xxvi.26-29, St Mark xiv.22-25, St Luke xxii.15-20) put it at the Passover itself. St John (xiii.1-xvii.26) has it the day before but all Gospels make this link between the Passover, the Last Supper and the Crucifixion. St Paul also makes this link abundantly clear in I Corinthians v.

Crucifixion.[203] In so doing Our Lord demonstrates that His death is to be a sacrifice on behalf of all mankind. St Paul says

> And walk in love, as Christ also hath loved us, and hath given himself for us an offering and a sacrifice to God for a sweetsmelling savour.[204]

This sacrifice is a sin-offering performed by Jesus as the high priest,[205] it is a single sacrifice,[206] and in this sin-offering, part of the blood is sprinkled before the temple veil and the rest poured on the altar,[207] and part of the sacrifice is consumed by God and by the priests.[208] The altar on which the blood is poured represents God and thus the pouring of the blood of the sacrifice signifies the restoration of the covenant between God and Man. The sacrificial victim, of course, stands for the guilty party.

Indeed, by timing this sacrifice with Passover which everyone had to eat, for this was the sacrifice of deliverance from slavery in Egypt, Jesus is the Passover Lamb that was slain and

> Worthy is the Lamb that was slain to receive power, and riches, and wisdom, and strength, and honour, and glory, and blessing.[209]

This establishes that the Crucifixion of Our Lord is a sacrifice for sins and for the deliverance and salvation of humanity. It has also been established that Our Lord is both priest and sacrifice, and that He offers Himself upon the Cross which becomes the altar of this sacrifice. Further, from the words of the Lord and the nature of both the Passover and the sin-offering, all people receive the flesh of the sacrifice and Jesus tells His followers that they must eat and drink of His body and blood. Lastly, it has been established from the letter to the Hebrews that this is a single, unrepeated sacrifice. This raises a question. If this is all true then how it is possible for all people of two thousand years' distance to take part fully in this sacrifice for the remission of sins, even down to the consumption of the victim?

---

[203] This is why Easter is often called the Paschal Mystery after the Hebrew פֶּסַח (*pesah*) for Passover.
[204] Ephesians v.2
[205] Hebrews vii.24-28
[206] Hebrews ix.24-26
[207] Leviticus iv
[208] Leviticus vi.24-30
[209] Revelation v.12

As God commands these sacrifices in the Torah, it is clear that He expects these sacrifices to be fulfilled in Christ even down to the last tittle.[210] There can be only one answer: Our Lord gives Christians His Body and Blood to consume. This means that the Mass is not *a* sacrifice: it has to be precisely *the same* sacrifice as the Last Supper AND the same sacrifice as the Crucifixion. When Christians are present at Mass, they are participating in this same single sacrifice. This is why it is a true communion: it is the communion of the Church across time as well as space and a folding of created reality beyond into eternity.

As was posited above, this may defy the purely rational and materialist senses and their understanding of the world around, but it does point to God's sheer mastery over the whole cosmos and the depths that it possesses beyond all the techniques of the empirical sciences. This is the why having faith is necessary in approaching conclusions that are correct in theological science but are not apparent to any sensible science.

This is all very well. Reason has been used based on Scripture to arrive at this conclusion. Is this conclusion supported by the Church Fathers?

St Cyril instructs the new Christians preparing for their baptism that the Mass is indeed a sacrifice, though no new blood has to be spilled:

> Then, after the spiritual sacrifice, the bloodless service, is completed, over that sacrifice of propitiation we entreat God for the common peace of the Churches, for the welfare of the world; for kings; for soldiers and allies; for the sick; for the afflicted; and, in a word, for all who stand in need of succour we all pray and offer this sacrifice.[211]

St Clement argues that there needs to be respect for those who offer the "gifts"[212] which does give the first hint that the Church has already regarded the Mass as a sacrifice in the first few decades after the Crucifixion. St Irenaeus certainly reinforces this, demonstrating that the duty of sacrifice has passed from the Jews to the Christians.[213] St Cyprian tells a tale about the Mass during the persecution of Christians in the third century[214] in which he refers to the Mass as a sacrifice which is joined to the Crucifixion, and that those who partake of this sacrifice take both the

---

[210] St Matthew v.18
[211] St Cyril of Jerusalem, Catechetical Lectures xxiii.8 (NPNF2, VII, p 154)
[212] St Clement of Rome, I Corinthians xliv (ANF, I, p 17)
[213] St Irenaeus, Against Heresies IV, xvii.5 (ANF, I, p 484) and xviii.2 (ANF, I, p 484-485)
[214] St Cyprian, Treatise III, On the Lapsed, xxv (ANF, V, p444)

bread and wine as Body and Blood. St John Chrysostom is even clearer in this link between the Mass and the Sacrifice on the Cross:

> What then? Do not we offer every day? We offer indeed, but making a remembrance of His death, and this [remembrance] is one and not many. How is it one, and not many? Inasmuch as that [Sacrifice] was once for all offered, [and] carried into the Holy of Holies. This is a figure of that [sacrifice] and this remembrance of that. For we always offer the same, not one sheep now and tomorrow another, but always the same thing: so that the sacrifice is one. And yet by this reasoning, since the offering is made in many places, are there many Christs? But Christ is one everywhere, being complete here and complete there also, one Body. As then while offered in many places, He is one body and not many bodies; so also [He is] one sacrifice. He is our High Priest, who offered the sacrifice that cleanses us. That we offer now also, which was then offered, which cannot be exhausted. This is done in remembrance of what was then done. For (says He) *do this in remembrance of Me*.[215] It is not another sacrifice, as the High Priest, but we offer always the same, or rather we perform a remembrance of a Sacrifice. [216]

Further, in the Sacramentary of St Serapion (fl 330-360), this one sacrifice is very evident and written into the very canon of the Mass.[217]

It can be readily seen that there is reasonable, scriptural and traditional support for this teaching and can be concluded that the Mass is indeed a participation in Christ's single sacrifice made once for all upon the Cross. Every single Mass brings the congregation back to that very moment and unites Christians with every Mass that has been said, is being said, or shall be said.

> The Offering is the same, whether a common man [i.e. common priest], or Paul or Peter offer it. It is the same which Christ gave to His disciples, and which the Priests now minister. This is nowise inferior to that, because it is not men that sanctify even this, but the Same who sanctified the one sanctifies the other also. For as the words which God spoke are the same which the Priest now utters, so is the Offering the same, and the Baptism, that which He gave. Thus the whole is

---

[215] St Luke xxii.19
[216] St John Chrysostom, Homily on Hebrews xvii.6
[217] Anaphora of the Euchologion of Serapion. (Wobbermin, 1899) p 60

> of faith. The Spirit immediately fell upon Cornelius, because he had previously fulfilled his part, and contributed his faith. And this is His Body, as well as that. And he who thinks the one inferior to the other, knows not that Christ even now is present, even now operates.[218]

This may sound just as incomprehensible as the Doctrine of the Holy Trinity, but this is the reality that the Church is given by the sheer transcendence of Almighty God and it is no less credible than the doctrine of the Holy Trinity. The Mass is truly Holy Communion of the Church with Our Lord Jesus Christ throughout all Time and Space in which the atoning sacrifice is made and in which all Christians may participate.

The Necessity of the Priesthood

There is a third aspect of communion which St Ignatius mentions quite specifically. The Catholic Church believes that Our Lord is really present in the Sacrament and that every Christian who receives communion truly consumes the Body and Blood of Christ and, further that every Mass is inextricably and intimately linked with Our Lord's sacrifice as both priest and victim. If Christ the victim is really present then what of Christ the priest who offers the sacrifice on behalf of the congregation?

Again, following the above reasoning from the Epistle to the Hebrews shows that Our Lord must be really present in the person of the priest saying Mass as well. There are several deep mysteries here: the Real Presence, the True Communion of the Church united in one Mass, and even the mystery of God whose being transcends human ideas of identity and personhood. These deep ideas and their mysterious content have been backed up using the Catholic principles and so it is now necessary to do so in examining the idea of Christ being present in the priest at Mass. If this is true, then the priest is said to be acting *in persona Christi* – in the person of Christ.

First, is there any incidence of the Apostles acting *in persona Christi*? The phrase is certainly Biblical, to wit, in the Latin version of St Paul's second letter to the Corinthians:

> *cui autem aliquid donatis et ego nam et ego quod donavi si quid donavi propter vos in persona Christi*

---

[218] St John Chrysostom, Homilies on II Timothy, II (NPNF1, XIII, p483)

> To whom ye forgive any thing, I forgive also: for if I forgave any thing, to whom I forgave it, for your sakes forgave I it in the person of Christ;[219]

In this, St Paul is acting as a confessor in the Sacrament of Confession and is thus acting as a conduit for Our Lord's forgiveness. This shows that it is Biblically *possible* for a priest to act *in persona Christi*. There are three areas where clarification is required.

First, the words *in persona Christi* are a Latin translation of ἐν προσώπῳ Χριστοῦ – in the face of Christ, i.e. in His presence. Does this disqualify the idea of *in persona Christi* as the priest acting in the person of Christ? The Latin word *persona* is literally a mask, something through which a sound is made – *per sona*. It represents the authority of Christ who is described as a Person of the Trinity. Though this is a more technical use of the word Person, we understand it better when we refer to Jesus as the Word made flesh and thus, in His humanity bears the "sound of God" inextricably. When St Paul forgives sins *in persona Christi,* he becomes Christ by becoming the mask through which Christ speaks. In this sense, he decreases so that Christ can increase,[220] i.e. become present to those who are looking to meet Him.

Second, this is in the context of confession. How does this apply to Eucharist? It is possible for the priest to act *in persona Christi* and thus it is reasonable that Christ the Priest becomes present through the priest in order to sacrifice Christ the Victim in that single transcendent sacrifice of the Mass. There is also evidence that Apostles worked miracles through the power and authority of Christ.

> Now Peter and John went up together into the temple at the hour of prayer, being the ninth hour. And a certain man lame from his mother's womb was carried, whom they laid daily at the gate of the temple which is called Beautiful, to ask alms of them that entered into the temple; Who seeing Peter and John about to go into the temple asked an alms. And Peter, fastening his eyes upon him with John, said, Look on us. And he gave heed unto them, expecting to receive something of them. Then Peter said, Silver and gold have I none; but such as I have give I thee: In the name of Jesus Christ of Nazareth rise up and walk. And he took him by the right hand, and lifted him up: and immediately his feet and ankle bones received strength.[221]

---

[219] II Corinthians ii.10
[220] C.f. St John iii.30
[221] Acts iii.1-8

This gives good grounds to suppose that the priest acts in the person of Christ at the Mass.

Third, there are no further instances in the Bible of the Mass being celebrated to draw any further conclusions. It has only been asserted that the idea of the priest being *in persona Christi* is likely. Yet, the Mass has been celebrated in Biblical times without being recorded. This does mean that Tradition – that which is handed down to the Church alongside the Scriptures – is most valuable here. Is there any evidence for the priest acting *in persona Christi* in sacred Tradition?

St Cyprian views the Mass with all the gravity of a commandment.

> But if we may not break even the least of the Lord's commandments, how much rather is it forbidden to infringe such important ones, so great, so pertaining to the very Sacrament of our Lord's passion and our own redemption, or to change it by human tradition into anything else than what was divinely appointed! For if Jesus Christ, our Lord and God, is Himself the chief priest of God the Father, and has first offered Himself a sacrifice to the Father, and has commanded this to be done in commemoration of Himself, certainly that priest truly discharges the office of Christ, who imitates that which Christ did; and he then offers a true and full sacrifice in the Church to God the Father, when he proceeds to offer it according to what he sees Christ Himself to have offered.[222]

What St Cyprian effectively has said is that the priest is acting in full authority of Christ. Is the Mass merely an imitation of Christ's sacrifice? No, because he offers this "true and full sacrifice". St Ambrose is even stronger in this belief.

> We saw the Prince of Priests coming to us, we saw and heard Him offering His blood for us. We follow, inasmuch as we are able, being priests; and we offer the sacrifice on behalf of the people. And even if we are of but little merit, still, in the sacrifice, we are honourable. For even if Christ is not now seen as the one who offers the sacrifice, nevertheless it is He Himself that is offered in sacrifice here on earth when the body of Christ is offered. Indeed, to offer Himself He is made visible in us, he whose word makes holy the sacrifice that is offered.[223]

---

[222] St Cyprian of Carthage, Epistle LXII to Caecilius xiv (ANF, V, p 362)
[223] St Ambrose, Commentaries on the Psalms, Psalm xxxvii.25 (FEF II, ¶1260, p 150)

The priest is the conduit of Christ's presence as the Priest of the great Sacrifice. St John Chrysostom is in agreement here.

> Christ is present. The One [Christ] who prepared that [Holy Thursday] table is the very One who now prepares this [altar] table. For it is not a man who makes the sacrificial gifts become the Body and Blood of Christ, but He that was crucified for us, Christ Himself. The priest stands there carrying out the action, but the power and the grace is of God, "this is my body," he says. This statement transforms the gifts.[224]

Anglican Catholics have good grounds then to believe what Reason explains. Just as the bread and wine are consecrated into the Body and Blood of Christ, the priest, acting *in persona Christi* is an ikon, a depiction of the actions of Christ in whose authority he acts through the grace that he received at his Ordination.

The Priesthood

The priesthood is at the heart of Ignatian Catholicism and thus deserves to be looked at with greater scrutiny if Anglican Catholicism can claim to be Catholic in the Ignatian sense.

St Ignatius' understanding of practical Catholicism says that the central focus of the Church is on the person of the Bishop: no worshipping community can be properly regarded as Catholic without the Episcopate and, in particular, an Episcopate that is linked intrinsically with the sacraments.

The Priesthood Intended

Many Evangelical Christians say that it was not the Lord's intention to ordain anyone as clergy. On the contrary, there is ample evidence that He did, given the system of Sacraments that Jesus Himself gave to the Church through the sanctifying influence of His same presence, and His desire for all people to find the grace of God in the Church. Returning to St Ignatius of Antioch, writing at the very beginning of the second century, the offices of bishop, priest and deacon are already well-established within seventy years of Our Lord's Resurrection:

> Be on your guard, therefore, against such persons [heretics]. And this will be the case with you if you are not puffed up, and continue in intimate union with Jesus Christ our God, and the

---

[224] St John Chrysostom, Homilies on Treachery of Judas I.vi (FEF II, ¶1157, p 104)

bishop, and the enactments of the apostles. He that is within the altar is pure, but he that is without is not pure; that is, he who does anything apart from the bishop, and presbytery, and deacons, such a man is not pure in his conscience.[225]

Indeed, St Ignatius writes several times in his epistles about the threefold ministry of bishop, presbyter (i.e. priest), and deacon. This is confirmed by St Clement of Alexandria:

> Since, according to my opinion, the grades here in the Church, of bishops, presbyters, deacons, are imitations of the angelic glory, and of that economy which, the Scriptures say, awaits those who, following the footsteps of the apostles, have lived in perfection of righteousness according to the Gospel. [226]

Again, to say that Our Lord did not intend to extend His priesthood through ordained clergy would suggest that the Church erred very early on. Evangelicals owe as much to these first clergymen as much as any other Christian: disdaining the ministry of these first priests is rather like cutting off the branch on which every Christian sits!

This intention is very clear: following Holy Scripture and writers like St Ignatius, St Clement and St Hippolytus, the Church has authority and the mandate to ordain three orders of minister: bishop, priest and deacon.

Levi and Melchisedek[227]

What exactly is priesthood? This not as easy a question to answer as it might appear. During Our Lord's ministry on earth, there is a very obvious priesthood centred on the temple in Jerusalem. This is because there is a clear system of sacrifices that the priests are to perform on behalf of the people. At this point, it might be asked, "why can the people not just do that for themselves?" In order to make an answer to this, it is necessary to explain the context in which the priesthood sits.

The priesthood of the temple comes from the so-called Levitical priesthood. This priesthood is descended from Aaron who was a member of the old Jewish tribe of Levi. In Exodus, God's purpose for Aaron and his family may be seen:

---

[225] St Ignatius of Antioch, Epistle to the Trallians, vii (shorter version) (ANF I, p68-9)
[226] St Clement of Alexandria, Stromata VI,xiii (FEF I, ¶427 p184)
[227] There are several variants of the spelling of this priest-king's name. The spelling given by the source is preserved at the expense of consistency.

> And take thou unto thee Aaron thy brother, and his sons with him, from among the children of Israel, that he may minister unto me in the priest's office, even Aaron, Nadab and Abihu, Eleazar and Ithamar, Aaron's sons.[228]

Exodus xxix forms a detailed account of Aaron's consecration as priest and it may be inferred from this that this priesthood is hereditary and restricted to the tribe of Levi.[229] This Levitical priesthood was to offer sacrifices on behalf of the people, to assist unclean people to become clean, to bless, collect the tithes and offerings, as well as to teach and judge according to the Torah – the Law. It was also male in character.

There is, however, another priesthood mentioned in the Old Testament – that of Melchisedek.

> And Melchizedek king of Salem brought forth bread and wine: and he was the priest of the most high God. And he blessed him, and said, Blessed be Abram of the most high God, possessor of heaven and earth: And blessed be the most high God, which hath delivered thine enemies into thy hand. And he gave him tithes of all.[230]

This clearly predates Aaron, indeed this seems to be a completely different priesthood. Psalm cx speaks of the prefigured Christ, "Thou art a priest for ever after the order of Melchisedech."[231] In reference to this, the Letter to the Hebrews sets out the distinction between the two priesthoods and shows why Our Lord's priesthood according to the order of Melchisedek fulfils and subsumes the priesthood of Aaron.

If therefore perfection were by the Levitical priesthood, (for under it the people received the law,) what further need was there that another priest should rise after the order of Melchisedec, and not be called after the order of Aaron?[232]

The reasoning of the previous section has demonstrated that Our Lord is both priest and victim in the Sacrifice of the Altar. It is clear that this priesthood is of greater power than that of the Levitical priesthood.

> But Christ being come an high priest of good things to come , by a greater and more perfect tabernacle, not made with

---

[228] Exodus xxviii.1
[229] Deuteronomy x.8
[230] Genesis xiv.18-20
[231] Psalm cx.4
[232] Hebrews vii.11

hands, that is to say, not of this building; Neither by the blood of goats and calves, but by his own blood he entered in once into the holy place, having obtained eternal redemption for us. For if the blood of bulls and of goats, and the ashes of an heifer sprinkling the unclean, sanctifieth to the purifying of the flesh: How much more shall the blood of Christ, who through the eternal Spirit offered himself without spot to God, purge your conscience from dead works to serve the living God?[233]

What is to be made of this? Given this and the commandment of the Lord that Christians should all receive His Body and Blood in the Sacrament of the Mass, it shows that Our Lord intended that there should be a priesthood for the Church. Just as He perfects the sacrificial victim, so does He perfect the priesthood.

In his major treatise on the dignity of the priesthood, St John Chrysostom speaks about the difference between the Levitical and Christian priesthood.[234] Thus the Christian priesthood can be seen to be an eternal priesthood because Our Lord is a priest forever after the order of Melchisedek. Yet Our Lord faces the same problem as He does with His Sacrifice. The Christian can receive His Body and Blood through the Eucharist because all celebrations of the Eucharist are figments in time of the one Eucharist. The priest acts *in persona Christi* at the Eucharist by participating in Christ's Eternal priesthood and thus the Christian priesthood has some far-reaching consequences.

Function and Character

There is a consistent theme in the ministry of Our Lord: He has a tendency to sanctify things just by His very person. This is very typical of God who blurs the line between being and doing. Just as the Lord sanctifies the waters of Baptism by being baptised; just as He sanctifies unction by being anointed; just as He sanctifies Marriage by participating and blessing the wedding in Cana so He sanctifies humanity by being born and participating in the business of being human. And why? He participates in humanity so that human beings may participate in His Divinity.

If the Lord suffuses action with being then this has implications for the priesthood. The priesthood becomes less a role to fulfil by action, but rather seeks to make Christ the priest present by the simple act of being. The transformation of the Apostles after the Day of Pentecost is strikingly relevant here as we saw above.[235]

---

[233] Hebrews ix.12-14
[234] St John Chrysostom, On the Priesthood III,vi (NPNF1, XI, p46 -47)
[235] Acts iii.1-7

The disciples have been transformed from being men who sit at Our Lord's feet to being apostles whose very shadow imparts the power of Christ.[236] Their ordination has imparted something very clear to their character through various gifts from God:

> In like manner, let all reverence the deacons as an appointment of Jesus Christ, and the bishop as Jesus Christ, who is the Son of the Father, and the presbyters as the sanhedrin of God, and assembly of the apostles. Apart from these, there is no Church. Concerning all this, I am persuaded that you are of the same opinion. For I have received the manifestation of your love, and still have it with me, in your bishop, whose very appearance is highly instructive, and his meekness of itself a power; whom I imagine even the ungodly must reverence, seeing they are also pleased that I do not spare myself.[237]
>
> The bread again is at first common bread; but when the mystery sanctifies it, it is called and actually becomes the Body of Christ. So too the mystical oil [used in the Sacraments of baptism, confirmation, and for the sick], so too the wine; if they are things of little worth before the blessing, after their sanctification by the Spirit each of them has its own superior operation. The same power of the word also makes the priest venerable and honourable, separated from the generality of men by the blessing bestowed upon him [holy orders--laying on of hands]. Yesterday he was but one of the multitude, one of the people; suddenly he is made a guide, a president, a teacher of piety, an instructor in hidden mysteries.[238]
> Wherefore it is incumbent to obey the presbyters who are in the Church—those who, as I have shown, possess the succession from the apostles; those who, together with the succession of the episcopate, have received the certain gift of truth, according to the good pleasure of the Father.[239]

This does indicate that there has been a change in the character of one ordained bishop that is different from the layperson. The charge is always to venerate those in Holy Orders because each one bears that ikonographic image of Christ. Any

---

[236] Acts v.15
[237] St Ignatius of Antioch, Epistle to the Trallians iii (ANF, I, p 67)-
[238] St Gregory of Nyssa, Sermon on the Day of Lights or the Baptism of Christ (FEF II, ¶1062 p 58-59)
[239] St Irenaeus of Lyons, Against Heresies Book IV, xxvi.2 (ANF, I, p 497)

reverence paid to bishop, priest or deacon is paid directly to Christ, and not to the person of the clergyman. The clergyman who seeks the veneration for himself is committing a gross sin because he is stealing that which is due to Christ Himself. Following the above quotation, St Irenaeus continues that the "primitive succession" is vital to the unity and integrity of the Church.

This is why the ACC, as in the Church of Rome and of the East, refers to priests as "Father" and bishops as "My Lord." This does not contravene St Matthew xxiii.9 because the venerable titles belong not to the clergyman but to God alone and recognise that presence in the parish and diocese. St Benedict makes this point quite clear in the context of Abbots:

> An Abbot who is worthy to be over a monastery should always remember what he is called, and live up to the name of Superior. For he is believed to hold the place of Christ in the monastery, being called by a name of His, which is taken from the words of the Apostle: "You have received a Spirit of adoption as sons, by virtue of which we cry, 'Abba—Father!'[240]"[241]

St Cyril of Jerusalem also makes this point in his lectures to those about to be baptised.[242]

The grace given at ordination therefore transforms the recipient into a living ikon of Christ, despite his imperfections. Just as the wood on which an ikon is painted can be blemished with knots and strange patterns, so the recipient's own fallen human nature is given grace to bear the imprint of Christ. This imprint allows the priest to administer the Sacraments by virtue of God's grace – to wit, His active presence in the man. Thus the Levitical Priesthood and Christian/Melchisedek Priesthood may be compared:

- This Levitical priesthood was to offer sacrifices on behalf of the people, though these were in nature temporary: the Christian priesthood offers up the one sacrifice of all ages on behalf of the Church in the Holy Eucharist which is the actual Bread of Eternal Life.

- The Levitical priesthood was to assist unclean people to become clean: the Christian priesthood actually cleanses people by the Sacraments of Baptism and Confession.

---

[240] Romans viii.15
[241] St Benedict of Nursia, The Rule, ii, (McCann, 1952) p 17
[242] St Cyril of Jerusalem, Catechetical Lecture VII.ix (NPNF2, VII, p 46)

- The Levitical priesthood was to bless: the Christian priesthood is to pronounce God's actual joining of those married.

- The Levitical priesthood was to collect the tithes and offerings: the Christian priesthood is to receive and consecrate people's whole lives offered by confirmation with the Holy Ghost and through the Sacrament of Ordination.

- The Levitical priesthood was to teach and judge according to the Torah: the Christian priesthood is to hold to the fullness of the Catholic Faith as revealed in the Church through Holy Scripture, Holy Tradition and Right Reason.

Further to this, as Aaron and Moses had the objective presence of God in the great cloud, the Christian priesthood is the objective presence of God in the Church. Again, this is not to exalt the person of the priest in himself, but it becomes a great burden that he must bear not to his credit, but rather for the good of the whole Church.

Thus, according to Ignatian Catholicism, the function of a clergyman is intrinsically bound up in the character that he received from his ordination.

The Apostolic Succession

The laying on of hands is always significant in the New Testament. Whereas in the Old Testament, physical contact is always withheld from the ritually unclean, the laying on of hands, especially to the sick, again shows the tactile presence of Our Lord Jesus Christ to be life-giving, life-hallowing and life-changing.

Our Lord lays His hands on children,[243] and on the sick,[244] in acts of blessing and healing. Our Lord's touch confers power – even passively.[245] It is precisely this method that the Apostles use to confer the power of the Holy Ghost for the purpose for which they intend it. This includes healing following the example of the Lord[246] and, most pertinently, the ordination of deacon,[247] bishops and priests.[248]

---

[243] St Matthew xix.15
[244] St Luke iv.40; St Luke xiii.13
[245] St Matthew ix.20-22
[246] Acts xxviii.8
[247] Acts vi.6
[248] Acts xiii.3

The idea that Holy Orders are passed from bishop to bishop is already present by the time of St Irenaeus of Lyons who lives far enough from the first century to see that the tradition has become established and yet is still within "touching distance" of the apostles through his teacher, St Polycarp.

> It is within the power of all, therefore, in every Church, who may wish to see the truth, to contemplate clearly the tradition of the apostles manifested throughout the whole world; and we are in a position to reckon up those who were by the apostles instituted bishops in the Churches, and [to demonstrate] the succession of these men to our own times; those who neither taught nor knew of anything like what these [heretics] rave about. For if the apostles had known hidden mysteries, which they were in the habit of imparting to "the perfect" apart and privily from the rest, they would have delivered them especially to those to whom they were also committing the Churches themselves. For they were desirous that these men should be very perfect and blameless in all things, whom also they were leaving behind as their successors, delivering up their own place of government to these men; which men, if they discharged their functions honestly, would be a great boon [to the Church], but if they should fall away, the direst calamity.[249]

It is clear that this laying on of hands was to provide the means by which the clergy could continue throughout history. St Timothy is told, "lay hands suddenly on no man, neither be partaker of other men's sins: keep thyself pure." From this, we can see that discernment is of vital importance and that clergy are not to be ordained without some clear understanding that they are God's choice to receive the orders. St Hippolytus demonstrates that the imposition of hands is necessary for the conferring of Holy Orders by a bishop.[250] St Cyprian writes about the ordination of some dubious characters, Basilides and Martialis, and in so doing demonstrates how the Church has continued the method of the Sacrament.[251]

From these it can be seen that a bishop who goes off on a frolic of his own cannot be a source of unity, nor espouse the Catholic Faith. Already here, there is a clear direction that the faithful must dissociate themselves from heretical bishops. This is an issue that is responsible for the Continuing Anglican Movement and the emergence of the ACC from the canonical authority of the Anglican Communion.

---

[249] St Irenaeus of Lyons, Against Heresies, III.iii.1 (ANF I, p 415)
[250] St Hippolytus of Rome, The Apostolic Tradition ii (FEF I, ¶¶ 394a,b,c, p166-168)
[251] St Cyprian of Carthage, Epistle LXVII 3,4,5 (ANF V, p370)

Anglican Catholicism and Ignatian Catholicism

Since it has been demonstrated that the ACC is Catholic in the Cyrillic-Vincentian sense, it should follow that it is also Catholic in the Ignatian sense. It is of course possible that there is a form of "lip-service" whereby one side of Catholicism is emphasised at the expense of the other. Therefore, it is important to shore up any potential discrepancy between the two terms. What must the ACC do to demonstrate that it is Catholic in the Ignatian sense? Again, St Ignatius says:

Wherever the bishop shall appear, there let the multitude of the people also be; even as, wherever Jesus Christ is, there is the Catholic Church. It is not lawful without the bishop either to baptize or to celebrate a love-feast; but whatsoever he shall approve of, that is also pleasing to God, so that everything that is done may be secure and valid.

Thus, it must be established that the ACC possesses valid bishops around whom the congregation gather for the sacrament of communion with Christ.

Eucharistic Theology as the Locus of Communion

The Affirmation of St Louis states the Anglican Catholic belief in the Eucharist as "the sacrifice which unites us to the all-sufficient sacrifice of Christ on the Cross and the Sacrament in which He feeds us with His Body and Blood."[252] From this, it can be seen clearly that the ACC believes the Mass to be a participation in the single atoning sacrifice of Our Lord, that it is the locus of communion in that it unites Christians to Christ and thus to each other, and that Christians are fed with the Body and Blood of Christ. While this does not explicitly conform to the doctrine of the Real Presence as expounded above, the commitment of the ACC to the liturgy of the Book of Common Prayer in its 1549 and 1928 (US) editions makes the affirmation of the doctrine as found in the Prayer of Humble Access. The two versions are slightly different. The 1549 Prayer of Humble Access proceeds thus:

> We do not presume to come to this thy table (o mercifull lord) trusting in our owne righteousnes, but in thy manifold and great mercies: we be not woorthie so much as to gather up the cromes under thy table: but thou art the same lorde whose propertie is always to have mercie: Graunt us therefore (gracious lorde) so to eate the fleshe of thy dere sonne Jesus Christ, and to drynke his bloud in these holy Misteries, that we may continuallye dwell in hym, and he in us, that our synfull

---

[252] Affirmation of St Louis, ii

bodyes may bee made cleane by his body, and our soules washed through hys most precious bloud. Amen.

The 1928 American Prayer Book follows the 1662 book:

> WE do not presume to come to this thy Table, O merciful Lord, trusting in our own righteousness, but in thy manifold and great mercies. We are not worthy so much as to gather up the crumbs under thy Table. But thou art the same Lord, whose property is always to have mercy: Grant us therefore, gracious Lord, so to eat the flesh of thy dear Son Jesus Christ, and to drink his blood, that our sinful bodies may be made clean by his Body, and our souls washed through his most precious Blood, and that we may evermore dwell in him, and he in us. Amen.

The Prayer of Humble Access is an original composition[253] by Thomas Cranmer based on the words of the Centurion,[254] the Syro-Phoenician Woman,[255] and Our Lord Himself.[256] What is striking is that there is an ambiguity in how this may be interpreted, largely because of a Catholic reading of St John's discourse in his sixth chapter. This ambiguity allows for the ACC to read the prayer in the light of the Church Fathers who have demonstrated their conviction that Christ is truly and objectively present in the consecrated elements. Thus, how Anglican Catholics practice the doctrine of the Real Presence can be found in the Rites approved for the Mass. From these, as above, the Eucharistic theology of the ACC can be seen in harmony with the Primitive Church.

In the Gregorian Canon, the priest prays:

> Come, O Sanctifier, Almighty and Eternal God, and bless, (here he signs the cross over the bread and wine) this sacrifice prepared for the glory of Thy holy Name.

And, later, just before the consecration with hands held over the bread and wine in the same manner as the Jewish priest holds his hands on the victim,[257] he says,

---

[253] Marion Hatchett, Commentary on the American Prayerbook, New York: Seabury Press, 1981. p. 382
[254] St Matthew viii.8
[255] St Mark vii.28
[256] St John vi.56
[257] Leviticus iv.4,15

> which oblation, we beseech thee, O Almighty God, in all things to make blessed, appointed, ratified, reasonable and acceptable, that unto us it may be the Body and Blood of thy most dearly beloved Son, our Lord Jesus Christ.

In the Eucharistic Canon of 1549, the priest says,

> Hear us, O merciful Father, we beseech thee; and with thy Holy Spirit and Word, vouchsafe to ble+ ss and sanc+ tify these thy gifts, and creatures of bread and wine, that they may be unto us the body and blood of thy most dearly beloved Son Jesus Christ. Who in the same night that he was betrayed: took bread, and when he had blessed, and given thanks: he brake it, and gave it to his disciples, saying: Take, eat, this is my body which is given for you, do this in remembrance of me.
>
> Likewise after supper he took the cup, and when he had given thanks, he gave it to them, saying: drink ye all of this, for this is my blood of the New Testament, which is shed for you and for many, for remission of sins: do this as oft as you shall drink it, in remembrance of me.

In both cases, a definite intention of the priest to make present the Body and Blood of Christ through the Holy Ghost can be seen, following St Cyril of Jerusalem's description. It is something that He did and something that the Catholic Church has always done at the Lord's commandment.

There has always been a disagreement over what actually happens at the consecration in answer to a very reasonable question. The bread and wine look the same before consecration as they do afterwards: what has actually changed? If Catholics believe in the Real Presence, what can they mean if there is no apparent transformation?

If there is an answer to this question, then it lies in the answer to the question: what does it mean to be real? There are many different philosophical approaches to what reality is. One popular philosophy is that of Aristotle who distinguishes the reality of things by what they are (their substance) and how they appear to their senses (their accidents). In the thirteenth century, St Thomas Aquinas deduces from Aristotle's understanding of Reality that the substance of the bread and wine (what they actually are) is changed while their accidents (what they appear to be) do not change, thus defining the Roman doctrine of Transubstantiation. The reason why they appear to be bread and wine after consecration is so that Christians cannot be accused of cannibalism: the flesh of God is not like the flesh of man.

It is a compelling and popular theory, but Aristotle's view of reality is not ostensibly found in Holy Scripture: Scripture is revealed Theology, not Metaphysical Philosophy. It may make sense to human thinking, but human thinking, as intimated above, is not perfect. A lack of subscription to Aristotle's thinking yields little reason to believe in Transubstantiation. Contrariwise, walking with Aristotle perhaps renders St Thomas Aquinas' logic more convincing.

The only view of reality that the Bible gives is that God is truly real and that the reality of Creation is contingent completely and solely on His existence. This does suggest that there is a level of reality that is invisible to human beings and human physics. Acceptance of the fact that Jesus Christ is the Son of God is also acceptance of His telling the truth that His body is meat indeed. This may indeed confound some philosophies and worldviews, especially the materialist worldview. Given that there is a Kantian aspect to the theory of physical existence implied by the development of Quantum Mechanics and its startling predictions on observations that have been tested at the subatomic level, there is something about matter that is inaccessible to human observation, especially when that very observation alters the state of what is being observed physically. While human experience is limited to extension in space and time, the existence of God and the continued life of those in eternity with Him suggest modes of existence which are neither truly time-like nor space-like even factoring in higher dimensions as one might posit using more sophisticated mathematical physics such as M-Theory. The existence of God breaks through this inaccessibility and unknowability to produce something that may be known (i.e. bread becomes Body, wine becomes Blood) yet must be utterly inaccessible to all physical enquiry.

Thus the nature of the transformation is a real change but it is physically unknowable how this happens. Through the Catholic Faith it can be inferred that it *does* happen: Our Lord Jesus Christ is objectively and sacramentally present under the appearance of bread and wine after consecration. He is as really present at the Mass as each individual in the congregation is – perhaps more so! Whatever theory of reality is selected to assist the *fides quaerens intellectum* it must be recognised to be limited and accepted that it may not be any more than a shadow on the cave wall. An Anglican Catholic is bound to accept the Real Presence of Christ, but not bound to any particular philosophy to explain it. This is what is meant by Anglican Catholics believing a *form* of Transubstantiation – there is an aspect in which the what-is-it-ness of the elements have been transformed into the what-is-it-ness of the Body and Blood of Christ. While this may seem vaguely Aristotelian, more than this no more can be said.

The Internal View of the Anglican Catholic Priesthood

On this point, the Affirmation of St Louis says:

> The Holy Orders of bishops, priests and deacons as the perpetuation of Christ's gift of apostolic ministry to His Church, asserting the necessity of a bishop of apostolic succession (or priest ordained by such) as the celebrant of the Eucharist -- these Orders consisting exclusively of men in accordance with Christ's Will and institution (as evidenced by the Scriptures), and the universal practice of the Catholic Church.[258]

Further, the ACC has the Ignatian view of bishops, priests and deacons written into its canons.[259]

Further still, an Anglican Catholic bishop is canonically regarded as high priest:

> *High Priestly Power of the Episcopal Order.*
> Every Diocesan Bishop or Bishop Ordinary shall be faithful in admitting persons into Holy Orders and in celebrating the rite of confirmation as often and in as many places as shall be convenient, and he shall provide, as much as in him lies, that in every place within his Diocese or other Jurisdiction there shall be sufficient Priests to minister God's Word and Sacraments to all the people that are therein.[260]

Thus, Anglican Catholic bishops exist as high priests, celebrate the Mass and unify congregations in keeping with St Ignatius' understanding. What must be established further is that the succession of bishops that the ACC claims to hold in common with the apostles is an unbroken line. This is not important in order to prove the validity of Anglican Catholic orders in the eyes of other Catholic Churches, especially the Roman Catholic Church, though this would be of benefit for the purposes of ecumenism and the quest for the visible unity of the Catholic Church in which Anglican Catholicism claims to participate. The unbroken succession is necessary for the sake of internal consistency and for preservation of the Communion of the Saints. According to the Vincentian Canon, it should be that a Catholic from the First

---

[258] Affirmation of St Louis, ii
[259] To wit, Canon 6.1.01 which cites St. Ignatius of Antioch's Epistle to the Trallians, §2, §8, and the Epistle to the Smyrnaeans, §§8 & 9.
[260] Canon 6.6.01 (d)

Millennium should be able to recognise the orders of an Anglican Catholic bishop. In this sense, Anglican Catholic orders would stand or fall with Roman Catholic orders from the Great Schism to the Reformation.

Thus there are three places to consider where the Apostolic Succession might be breached: the Great Schism, the Reformation and the Denver Consecrations.

The ACC and Orthodox Orders

The Great Schism produces a breach between Eastern Orthodoxy and Roman Catholicism. As Fr Andrew Damick points out,[261] Roman sacramental theology is concerned with the outward sign of the laying on of hands, a view which leads to the recognition of the validity but not the regularity of the *episcopi vagantes*. The Orthodox Church takes the view that the outward sign is not enough but that the Orthodox Faith must be held. This makes sense that the Orthodox Faith cannot see ordination as anything but a sacrament that binds Cyrillic-Vincentian Catholicism to Ignatian Catholicism.

For the Anglican Communion, there have been some statements about Anglican Orders by the Orthodox Church which suggest that the question of the validity of Anglican Orders are regarded by the Orthodox in the same way as they regard Roman Orders.

In 1922, the Oecumenical Patriarch Meletius wrote an encyclical to the Presidents of Particular Orthodox Churches. In it he has the following paragraphs.

1. That the ordination of Matthew Parker as Archbishop of Canterbury by four bishops is a fact established by history.

2. That in this and subsequent ordinations there are found in their fullness those orthodox and indispensable, visible and sensible elements of valid episcopal ordination - viz. the laying on of hands, the Epiclesis of the All-Holy Spirit and also the purpose to transmit the charisma of the Episcopal ministry.

3. That the orthodox theologians who have scientifically examined the question have almost unanimously come to the same conclusions and have declared themselves as accepting the validity of Anglican Orders.

---

[261] (Damick, 2011) p 92-93

4. That the practice in the Church affords no indication that the Orthodox Church has ever officially treated the validity of Anglican Orders as in doubt, in such a way as would point to the re-ordination of the Anglican clergy as required in the case of the union of the two Churches.[262]

There have been similar statements by other leaders in the Orthodox Church such as the Patriarch of Jerusalem in 1923,[263] the Archbishop of Cyprus in 1923[264] and the Patriarch of Alexandria in 1930.[265] Admittedly, little has been done to make progress on these views and some may indeed have rescinded their view in the light of the Anglican Communion ordaining women to the priesthood and episcopate.

Given the Anglican Catholic holds the same basis of the Catholic Faith as Eastern Orthodoxy, it is clear that the possibility exists of Anglican Catholicism and Orthodoxy becoming united as Churches in the future and that Anglican Catholic orders will (or should) be recognised as they are. If the ACC holds the Orthodox Faith, then it is only now necessary to show that it has the same orders as the Roman Catholic Church.

Apostolicae Curae and the ACC

Anglican Catholicism technically falls under the Patriarch of the West - the Pope. This patriarchy was established in the reign of Emperor Justinian I (527-565) and ratified in 692 at the Quinisext Council. Pope Sergius I, however, rejected the concept of patriarchy which was therefore signed only by the Eastern Bishops.[266] It is interesting to note that the Pope used the title of Patriarch of the West from the mid-nineteenth century to 2006 when it was suppressed by Pope Benedict XVI.[267]

Given that Anglican Catholics believe that they are both Catholic and Orthodox, they would regard it as sacrilege to deny what they have in order to convert to Orthodoxy or Roman Catholicism: this is precisely what those two churches demand for the establishment of communion. The trouble is that these churches are not in

---

[262] Patriarch Meletios of Constantinople, Encyclical on Anglican Orders
[263] Patriarch Damianos of Jerusalem, A letter to the Archbishop of Canterbury dated 12th March 1923
[264] Archbishop Cyril of Cyprus, A letter to the Patriarch of Constantinople
[265] Patriarch Meletios of Alexandria, A letter to the Archbishop of Canterbury
[266] NPNF2, XIV p356-357
[267] Report by Catholic News Agency:
https://www.catholicnewsagency.com/news/vatican_says_abandoned_papal_title_patriarch_of_the_west_was_unclear_obsolete

communion because of history. Anglican Catholics share a common history with the Roman Catholic Church at the Great Schism and so cannot be in communion with the East and, similarly, they share a common history with the Church of England at the schism in the sixteenth century and so cannot be in communion with Rome. These are really the only reasons for the lack of communion.

Of course, the Roman Catholic Church denies that the ACC has valid orders because it believes that Anglican orders are invalid. This is expressed in the famous Papal Bull, *Apostolicae Curae*, issued by Pope Leo XIII in 1896. Essentially, this Bull declares that Anglican Orders are "absolutely null and utterly void" because of defects of form and intention.

On the defect of form, Pope Leo says:

> Being fully cognisant of the necessary connection between faith and worship, between "the law of believing and the law of praying", under a pretext of returning to the primitive form, they corrupted the Liturgical Order in many ways to suit the errors of the reformers. For this reason, in the whole Ordinal not only is there no clear mention of the sacrifice, of consecration, of the priesthood (*sacerdotium*), and of the power of consecrating and offering sacrifice but, as We have just stated, every trace of these things which had been in such prayers of the Catholic rite as they had not entirely rejected, was deliberately removed and struck out.[268]

> In vain also has been the contention of that small section of the Anglican body formed in recent times that the said Ordinal can be understood and interpreted in a sound and orthodox sense. Such efforts, we affirm, have been, and are, made in vain, and for this reason, that any words in the Anglican Ordinal, as it now is, which lend themselves to ambiguity, cannot be taken in the same sense as they possess in the Catholic rite. For once a new rite has been initiated in which, as we have seen, the Sacrament of Order is adulterated or denied, and from which all idea of consecration and sacrifice has been rejected, the formula, "Receive the Holy Ghost", no longer holds good, because the Spirit is infused into the soul with the grace of the Sacrament, and so the words "for the office and work of a priest or bishop", and the like no longer

---

[268] Pope Leo XIII, *Apostolicae Curae* xxx

> hold good, but remain as words without the reality which Christ instituted.[269]

Essentially, Pope Leo is saying that, because there is no mention of the offices of priest or bishop, or of the idea of the sacrifice of the Mass in the prayers, the form of words used is insufficient as an imprecation for the Holy Ghost to do that which He has always done.

On the defect of intention, he says

> With this inherent defect of "form" is joined the defect of "intention" which is equally essential to the Sacrament. The Church does not judge about the mind and intention, in so far as it is something by its nature internal; but in so far as it is manifested externally she is bound to judge concerning it. A person who has correctly and seriously used the requisite matter and form to effect and confer a Sacrament is presumed for that very reason to have intended to do (*intendisse*) what the Church does. On this principle rests the doctrine that a Sacrament is truly conferred by the ministry of one who is a heretic or unbaptized, provided the Catholic rite be employed. On the other hand, if the rite be changed, with the manifest intention of introducing another rite not approved by the Church and of rejecting what the Church does, and what, by the institution of Christ, belongs to the nature of the Sacrament, then it is clear that not only is the necessary intention wanting to the Sacrament, but that the intention is adverse to and destructive of the Sacrament.[270]

Here he says that, because the Church of England has changed the rite of ordination, it does not intend to consecrate Catholic bishops, priests and deacons.

In countering this, it needs to be pointed out that the prayer book of 1662 contains the following at the laying of hands on bishop and priest:

> Receive the Holy Ghost for the office and work of a Bishop in the Church of God, now committed unto thee by the imposition of our hands; In the Name of the Father, and of the Son, and of the Holy Ghost. Amen. And remember that thou stir up the grace of God which is given thee by this imposition of our hands: for God hath not given us the spirit of fear, but of power, and love, and soberness.

---

[269] Pope Leo XIII, *Apostolicae Curae* xxxi
[270] Pope Leo XIII, *Apostolicae Curae*, xxxiii

> Receive the Holy Ghost for the office and work of a Priest in the Church of God, now committed unto thee by the imposition of our hands. Whose sins thou dost forgive, they are forgiven; and whose sins thou dost retain, they are retained. And be thou a faithful dispenser of the Word of God, and of his holy Sacraments; In the Name of the Father, and of the Son, and of the Holy Ghost. Amen.

The Preface of the 1550 Ordinal states quite clearly that leaving the authority of the Papacy did not mean that the Church of England saw itself as leaving the Catholic Church and there is some clear intention to do precisely what the Catholic Church has always done:

> It is evident unto all men, diligently reading Holy Scripture, and ancient authors, that from the Apostles' time, there hath been these orders of Ministers in Christ's church, Bishops, Priests, and Deacons, which Offices were evermore had in such reverent estimation, that no man by his own private authority, might presume to execute any of them, except he were first called, tried, examined, and known, to have such qualities, as were requisite for the same. And also by public prayer, with imposition of hands, approved, and admitted thereunto. And therefore to the intent these orders should be continued, and reverently used, and esteemed in this Church of England, it is requisite, that no man (not being at this present Bishop, Priest, nor Deacon) shall execute any of them, except he be called, tried, examined, and admitted, according to the form hereafter following.

Richard Hooker is clear that the Church of England intends to preserve the Apostolic Succession of bishops.[271] John Cosin also argues that Protestants who have rejected episcopacy have nullified their orders.[272]

If all this were not enough, Anglican Catholic bishops have had consecrators who have valid orders in the eyes of Roman Catholicism. Bishop Chambers himself had a bishop of the Polish National Catholic Church, namely Bishop Francis Rowinski, as one of his consecrators. Bishop Pagtakhan also had Old Catholic bishops in his episcopal succession. Indeed, the involvement of the Old Catholic Church in

---

[271] Richard Hooker, The Laws of Ecclesiastical Polity, VII, xiv.11 as cited in (More, et al., 1935) p 397
[272] John Cosin, Letter to Mr Cordel at Blois as cited in (More, et al., 1935) p 398

Anglican episcopal ordinations means that finding a bishop in the Anglican Communion without an Old Catholic in their line consecration is incredibly difficult.

Of course, Pope Leo might then say that they are still consecrating with the wrong form and thus the consecrations are still invalid. Pope Leo's logic may be right, but it is based on false premises. The preface to the Ordinal shows that the Church of England always intended to make bishops, priests and deacons in the manner from Apostolic times. The whole liturgy of consecration is based around this intention. It might be noted that the prayer of ordination for a priest does not mention the sacrifice of the Mass at all – does that constitute a defective form? Indeed, this is something Archbishops Temple and Maclagan put forward in their reply to Pope Leo:

Both however of these opinions are strange, inasmuch as in the most ancient Roman formulary used, as it seems, at the beginning of the third century after Christ (seeing that exactly the same form is employed both for a Bishop and a Presbyter, except the name), nothing whatever is said about "high priesthood" or "priesthood" nor about the sacrifice of the Body and Blood of Christ. "The prayers and oblations which he will offer (to God) by day and by night" are alone mentioned, and the power of remitting sins is touched on.[273]

The text *Saepius Officio* by these Archbishops clearly demonstrates that Pope Leo is gravely misinformed about the facts of Anglican Orders and that Anglican Orders always have been as valid as Roman Catholic ones. Although Cardinal Vaughan subsequently tried to vindicate the Papal argument, his vindication is meaningless in the light of the Old Catholic involvement in episcopal consecrations and with the regard held by the Orthodox Churches of the 1920s.

There is one further problem with Pope Leo's bull and this is caused by the change in the Ordination Rite following Vatican II. One interesting development about this is from the late Fr Anthony Cekada, a member of the Society of Saint Pius X, who has put forward the thesis that ordinations using the 1968 rite are invalid for much the same reasons as put forward in *Apostolicae Curae*.[274] If this is true then the modern Roman Catholic episcopate stands or falls with the Anglican episcopate. In his application of traditional Roman Sacramental theology – the same theology

---

[273] Archbishop Frederick Temple of Canterbury and Archbishop William Dalrymple Maclagan of York, *Saepius Officio* XII
[274] Rev. Anthony Cekada, Absolutely Null and Utterly Void: The 1968 Rite of Episcopal Consecration.
http://www.traditionalmass.org/images/articles/NewEpConsArtPDF2.pdf

familiar with Pius X and, presumably his immediate predecessor Leo XIII – he states:

> (8) The new form fails to meet two criteria for the form for Holy Orders laid down by Pius XII.
> (a) Because the term governing Spirit is capable of signifying many different things and persons, it does not univocally signify the sacramental effect.
> (b) It lacks any term that even equivocally connotes the power of Order that a bishop possess — the "fullness of the priesthood of Christ in the episcopal office and order," or "the fullness or totality of the priestly ministry."
> (9) For these reasons, the new form constitutes a substantial change in the meaning of the sacramental form for conferring the episcopacy.
> (10) A substantial change in the meaning of a sacramental form, as we have already demonstrated, renders a sacrament invalid.

This is the same argument that renders Anglican Orders null and void in *Apostolicae Curae* and one can either conclude that there have been no valid consecrations using the new rite or admit that *Apostolicae Curae* is in error. Thus, if the Roman Catholic line of succession is valid then the Anglican line of succession is as equally valid at least in the Ignatian sense.

It is also instructive to note that, in 1966, Pope Paul VI gave his episcopal ring to Dr Michael Ramsay, the Archbishop of Canterbury at the first public meeting between Roman and Anglican leaders since the Reformation. In 2016, Pope Francis gave the Archbishop of Canterbury, Justin Welby, an episcopal crosier. This does seem to suggest that there is some spirit stirring within the Roman Catholic Church with respect to challenging the findings of Pope Leo.

Conclusion

The goal of this chapter has been to demonstrate that the ACC is Catholic in the Ignatian sense. It has been established that the ACC has Cyrillic-Vincentian Catholicism written into its doctrine and this is necessary in order to demonstrate that Anglican Catholicism is truly Orthodox. In demonstrating that the official doctrine of the ACC is that of the objective Real Presence in a re-presentation of the Eucharistic Sacrifice, it may be seen that the Ignatian idea of communion is sound in Anglican Catholic theology.

Further, it has been shown that any breach with the Roman Catholic succession itself renders modern Roman Catholic orders null and void. Given that the Orthodox Church regards the tactile succession of both Roman and Anglican Catholic orders as equally sound, it seems more likely that the Roman theology of ordination is too reliant on Papal fiat and developments that have taken place since the Great Schism. Thus it seems more likely that Anglican Catholic orders are valid in Orthodox eyes than Roman Catholic orders given the rejection of Papal claims and a commitment to the doctrine of the Primitive Church. Even if in the unlikely event that Anglican Orders were not valid at the breach from Rome, the involvement of Old Catholic bishops in consecrating Anglican bishops – especially those involved in the Continuing Anglican movement – grants them that validity.

Thus, the Anglican Church is a communion of Christians who are in communion with their bishops who derive their ordination from the Apostles, and receive the sacraments from them. This goes a long way in establishing that the ACC is Catholic in the Ignatian sense and the Cyrillic-Vincentian sense and thus it may be seen to be well-named "Catholic". The next direction is to understand how the ACC understands Anglicanism.

Anglicanism and the ACC

The two chapters above have sought to demonstrate that the Anglican Catholic Church is indeed Catholic in the senses recognised by the Primitive Church. It is now necessary to look at how it considers itself to be Anglican and how this fits in with others who would thus describe themselves. This is no easy task since "Anglican" has come to mean different things to different people, and much heated dialogue takes place in answer to questions of Anglican identity. This potentially gives rise to an identity crisis.

For example, in the Church of England, neighbouring parishes can be radically different. Certainly before the erection of the Anglican Ordinariate within the Roman Catholic Church in 2011, one could find one Church of England parish using the *Novus Ordo* Roman Missal and the neighbouring parish holding a worship meeting in a local cinema. The observer might be fooled into thinking that one parish is Roman Catholic and the other an offshoot of a Pentecostal Megachurch. Between the two there seems little to identify either of them as being Anglican. They disagree about which doctrines to hold, what a priest is and who is eligible for ordination. These are, of course, extremes but they serve as an illustration of what the Church of England and the Anglican Communion are today. Indeed, in the introduction to the Handbook of Anglican Studies,[275] the very idea of the existence of Anglicanism is questioned by serious academics. It is no wonder that there have been attempts to reclaim some meaning of what Anglicanism is and thereby restore some sense of Anglican orthodoxy: this has resulted in churches breaking away (in an institutional sense) from the Anglican Communion.

The first to do so was the Free Church of England and its American counterpart, the Reformed Episcopal Church.[276] The former left the Church of England in 1844 in order to pursue a more Calvinist and rigorous adherence to the XXXIX Articles in reaction to the Oxford Movement's attempts to restore a more Catholic view to the Church of England. There have been other such bodies, like the Orthodox Anglican Church instituted in 1963. Crucially, these have been largely Evangelical Anglicans, i.e. who hold to the doctrine found in the XXXIX Articles. The Continuing Anglican Movement is largely the first to have been Anglo-Catholic in nature, though the

---

[275] (Chapman, et al., 2015) p 11
[276] While it might be tempting to see Methodism as the first major body to separate itself from the Anglican Church, it has to be said that these sought to adapt their heritage in line with their quest for personal holiness. The Free Church of England and its communion partners sought expressly to preserve the use of the Anglican Formularies.

United Episcopal Church which shares the ACC's origins now distances itself from the Affirmation of St Louis.

The ACC is often challenged on the nature of its Anglicanism. Often it is dismissed on the grounds that "an Anglican has to be in communion with the Archbishop of Canterbury" or "an Anglican has to be Protestant" or "an Anglican cannot use a Missal" et c. These questions raise deeper questions of identity. Is the ACC actually Protestant? Is the ACC justified walking apart from the Anglican Communion? Is the ACC a "real church" in the first place?

First, it is necessary to arrive at a definition of the word "Anglican" that at least seems coherent even to those that might fervently disagree.

The Question of Anglican Identity

Is it possible to make a definition of "Anglican" which an enquirer might understand and appreciate? Given the sheer complexity of the series of reformations that took place to the Church in the sixteenth and seventeenth centuries, the fact that the Church of England has sought to be comprehensive, i.e. patient of many different theologies within its ecclesiology, has created much confusion and even ill-feeling. The Rev. Paul Avis has provided a paper with the title "What is 'Anglicanism'?"[277] in which he searches for some coherence in the term. He quotes (p 474) Bishop Hensley Henson who admits:

> The doctrinal incoherence of the Church of England though it is unquestionably perplexing, practically embarrassing and not infrequently actually scandalous, has its roots in something far more respectable than an indolent acquiescence in undiscipline or reprehensible indifference to truth.[278]

Avis' conclusion is that Anglican identity lies within an Anglican "theological method and the understanding of authority that informs it, rather than in terms of liturgy, spirituality or polity."

Yet, Bishop Henry McAdoo contradicts this view:

> Anglicanism is not a theological system and there is no writer who is an essential part of it either in respect of content or with regard to the form of its self-expression [...]. The absence of

---

[277] (Sykes, et al., 1988) p 459 - 476
[278] Hensley Henson, The Church of England p 108

> an official theology in Anglicanism is something deliberate which belongs to its essential nature, for it has always regarded the teaching and practice of the undivided Church of the first five centuries as a criterion.[279]

It must also be said that, as has been shown, Roman Catholicism and Eastern Orthodoxy potentially have the same approach to authority, namely Scripture, Tradition and Right Reason albeit in distinct emphases and in different semantic frameworks. The difference is how these are enshrined in the life of these churches, be it the Magisterium with Pope as *vox ecclesiae* or the *consensus fidei* immutably expressed by the Councils. It might be understood from this that the Anglican Communion has no longer any centralising uniformity of doctrine but rather seems to be like a federation of congregations of different churchmanship within the oversight of bishops.

This is not to suggest that a desire for some deeper unity within the Anglican Communion is absent, far from it. The famous Chicago-Lambeth Quadrilateral states:

> As inherent parts of this sacred deposit, and therefore as essential to the restoration of unity among the divided branches of Christendom, we account the following, to wit:
>
> 1. The Holy Scriptures of the Old and New Testaments as the revealed Word of God.
> 2. The Nicene Creed as the sufficient statement of the Christian Faith.
> 3. The two Sacraments,--Baptism and the Supper of the Lord,--ministered with unfailing use of Christ's words of institution and of the elements ordained by Him.
> 4. The Historic Episcopate, locally adapted in the methods of its administration to the varying needs of the nations and peoples called of God into the unity of His Church.

Yet, this is not enough now that the presence of women in the episcopate is prevalent in, and disputed within, many of the provinces of the Anglican Communion. Even within the Church of England, there is a belief among members of Forward in Faith that the Historic Episcopate has been breached and thus that the sacrament of the Supper of the Lord has been correspondingly compromised.

---

[279] Henry McAdoo, The Spirit of Anglicanism p v. quoted in Robert Wright's paper, An Essay on Terminology (Sykes, et al., 1988) p 477 – 478, just a few pages from Avis' statement to the contrary.

The new prayer book revision of 2000 also brought into existence Common Worship to replace the Alternative Service Book of 1980 and act as a preferred compendium of liturgy over the 1662 Book of Common Prayer which, although certainly not forbidden and indeed rather regarded as normative, is largely ignored. Common Worship, as the official liturgical resource of the Church of England, presents different liturgies of the Mass[280] and even different Affirmations of Faith[281] to replace the Nicene Creed at Mass.[282] Thus, the diversity of prayer and understanding of communion within the Church of England shows that any commitment to *lex orandi lex credendi* produces a greater variety of Christian belief. Common Worship certainly does not rule out the Nicene Creed but there are congregations which are not exposed to it because it is not a regular part of their Sunday Mass.

It may be asked what may be regarded as "common" about Common Worship but reading the notes on the Eucharist reveals that the different Eucharistic prayers have a common structure. Indeed, the different prayers reflect more the ancient diversity of rites such as the liturgies of St James and St Basil and thus point to pre-Reformation celebration of the Mass rather than to something that many would regard as Anglican. It must be remembered that from 1549 onwards, only one liturgy of the Mass was permitted. Compare this with Archbishop Cranmer's preface to the 1549 Book of Common Prayer:

> And where heretofore, there hath been great diversitie in saying and synging in churches within this realme: some folowyng Salsbury use, some Herford use, same the use of Bangor, some of Yorke, and some of Lincolne: *Now from hencefurth, all the whole realme shall have but one use.* And if any would judge this waye more painfull, because that all thynges must be read upon the boke, whereas before, by the reason of so often repeticion, they could saye many thynges by heart: if those men will waye their labor, with the profite in

---

[280] There are eight Eucharistic prayers for Order One, and one more for Order Two. https://www.churchofengland.org/prayer-and-worship/worship-texts-and-resources/common-worship/holy-communion-service

[281] The pattern for four speculative churches is mentioned in discussion of the Affirmations of Faith. https://www.churchofengland.org/prayer-and-worship/worship-texts-and-resources/common-worship/common-material/new-patterns-28 (Accessed 23rd March 2021)

[282] Although, Common Worship does say (*ibid*) that the use of authorised affirmations of Faith is intended to be occasional, there is nothing to stop a parish relegating the use of the Nicene Creed to be honoured more in the breach than in the norm.

> knowlege, whiche dayely they shal obtein by readyng upon the boke, they will not refuse the payn, in consideracion of the greate profite that shall ensue therof.[283]

The question might be asked why this diversity in liturgy came about. The answer may probably be found in the practices of the Ritualists of the nineteenth century who sought to recover a more Catholic liturgy from the Book of Common Prayer.

If Anglicanism is committed to *lex orandi, lex credendi*, then there remains a question as to just what Anglican identity is if Cranmer's initial intention for commonality of worship has been rescinded.

Further, in discussing the theological position of the Church of England, Archbishop Fisher makes the famous comment

> We have no doctrine of our own – we only possess the Catholic doctrine of the Catholic Church, enshrined in the Catholic Creeds, and those Creeds we hold without addition or diminution... the Church, of England was in existence long before the Reformation, and while it was deeply affected by the travails of the Reformation, it emerged from them in all essential reflects the same Church, as before within the One Catholic and Apostolic Church...[284]

Certainly, the historical fact of the Church of England is that it sought to be comprehensive in keeping Lutheran and Calvinists together, perhaps even with the rump of Henrician "Catholics without the Pope" left isolated by the death of Mary I and who, until 1570 when the excommunication of Elizabeth and her church was promulgated, attended the services from the new order and may even have received the sacraments.[285] This comprehensiveness may yield a way of defining Anglicanism albeit in a less direct manner.

Anglicanism and Wittgenstein

According to his Philosophical Investigations, Ludwig Wittgenstein puts forward the idea of *Familienähnlichkeit*, i.e. the method of using "family resemblances" to

---

[283] Emphasis added.
[284] Archbishop Geoffrey Fisher, from a speech given at Central Hall, Westminster, Church Times, 2 February 1951
[285] (Walsham, 1993)

determine the nature of a concept. Wittgenstein uses this to determine what a game is,[286] and then says in the next section:

> I can think of no better expression to characterize these similarities than "family resemblances"; for the various resemblances between members of a family: build, features, colour of eyes, gait, temperament, etc. etc. overlap and criss-cross in the same way. – And I shall say: "games" form a family.

Given that the Church is supposed to be a family under the parentage of God Himself, it seems very apposite to use Wittgenstein's method to bolster and explore the understanding of Anglicanism as a family.

There are several traits that might come together to construct some form of Anglican identity. It might be said that a church possesses an Anglican Identity

1) by continuing in the Apostolic Succession with Anglican Bishops;

2) by the continued use of Scripture, Tradition and Right Reason in continuity with the great Anglican Divines – Hooker, Andrewes et al;

3) by worshipping in the same places or in the same buildings as antiquity such as the great cathedrals of England;

4) by being in communion with the Archbishop of Canterbury;

5) by being a Christian subject of the British Monarch in the capacity of Supreme Governor of the Church of England;

6) by adhering to traditional Anglican liturgies;

7) by seeking some *via media* between Roman Catholicism and Protestantism;

8) by taking the so-called Anglican Formularies (The Book of Common Prayer, the Ordinal, the XXXIX articles and the Homilies) as the basis of one's dogmatic system;

9) by being patient of *theologoumena*;

10) by rejecting the Universal Jurisdiction of the Pope;

---

[286] Ludwig Wittgenstein, Philosophical Investigations §66

11) by rejecting *Apostolicae Curae*.

These are all statements that have been used to give an impression as to what an Anglican Church looks like. Of course, some of them are rather moot: how can a member of ECUSA – a member church of the Anglican Communion – be a subject of the British Monarch? Is one an Anglican just by worshipping in St Agatha's Landport, which was a Church of England building but is now a flagship parish of the Anglican Ordinariate within the Roman Catholic Church?

Nonetheless, here is presented a set of characteristics which one might certainly see apply to the Church of England at least prior to the Alternative Service Book of 1980 which signified a clear, established movement away from the traditional liturgy of the Book of Common Prayer. Further, if there is truth to the idea that the ordination of women is not a valid sacrament then there are grounds for suggesting that the Apostolic Succession with Anglican Bishops has been broken by the Church of England and all who are in full communion with her. Certainly, that is the position of a minority within the Church of England. Nonetheless, the Church of England – the epitome of Anglicanism – has satisfied all these criteria at some stage in her history. Other members of the Anglican Communion have not held all of these positions and yet qualify as being Anglican and therefore the list must be sufficient to define what Anglicanism is but without many of them being logically necessary.

It is possible to see quite quickly that many of these statements apply to the ACC, albeit to varying degrees. The rejection of the authority of *Apostolicae Curae* has already been examined, as has the use of Scripture, Tradition and Reason as a basis of God's revelation. The Pope has no legal standing in the ACC as the absence of the Papal office from the Canons demonstrates clearly.

There are problems, too. The Affirmation of St Louis was drafted in 1977 and always had the intention of remaining in communion with Canterbury. It states clearly,

> We affirm our continued relations of communion with the See of Canterbury and all faithful parts of the Anglican Communion.

However, it was forced to add a footnote to this article:

> Because of the action of General Synod of the Church of England, Parliament, and the Royal Assent,[287] the Colleges of Bishops of the Churches of the Chamber's succession are

---

[287] That is, the assent to the ordination of women in 1992.

> obliged no longer to count the See of Canterbury as a faithful part of the Anglican Communion.

Thus, communion with the Archbishop of Canterbury is impossible and, for many members of the Church of England, this would rule Anglican Catholics out of being Anglican.

Further, there is the fact that the Anglican Formularies are blatantly hostile to doctrines which are clearly Catholic. The XXXIX Articles condemn the Real Presence of Christ in the Eucharistic elements and thus the rites of Exposition and Benediction,[288] the veneration of ikons, the invocation of the saints and synergism, as do the Homilies. Indeed, there are questions about how far the Anglican Formularies are authoritative and how they are to be read, especially when it comes to understanding the priesthood and the Apostolic Succession of bishops. Dr Bicknell states:

> The significance of our Articles may best be learnt by a comparison between them and the Creeds. Both are theological statements of belief. Both alike have been employed as tests. Both are attempts to preserve the truth in all its fulness. But while the Creeds are a necessity, 'in a world where all expression of spirit is through body,' Articles are a consequence 'not of the Church's existence but of the Church's failure.' 'The Church, without a Creed, would not in human life on earth, however ideally perfect, have been a Church at all. But if the Church on earth had been ideally perfect, or anything even remotely like it, there would never have been any 39 Articles, The one is a necessary feature of spiritual reality. The other is an unfortunate consequence of spiritual failure.'[289]

Bicknell, citing Dr Moberly, demonstrates that the Articles arose precisely as a reaction to the perceived errors of the Roman Catholic Church. They are not a Creed but essentially a clarification. That subscription to the Articles after 1571 was required by all clergymen and scholars shows that they were not given the status of a confession required of any layman.[290] Yet, for some ecclesial jurisdictions,[291] the

---

[288] The preferred Eucharistic Theology seems to be Receptionism – see William Crockett, Holy Communion, (Sykes, et al., 1988) p 309-301
[289] (Bicknell, et al., 1939) p23 citing R. C. Moberly, Problems and Principles, p 378-379
[290] (Browne, 1887) p11
[291] Such as the United Episcopal Church and the Church of England (Continuing)

need to enshrine the Articles in their constitution is crucial for their Anglican identity.

These are serious points and mean that any identity that the ACC shares with the historic Church of England must either be nuanced or entirely superficial. Clearly, the ACC has a different doctrine from the Church of England: how does this affect its qualification to Anglicanism?

The Anglican Succession of the ACC[292]

First, the ACC continues that which the Church of England continued at the Reformation. The ACC does indeed receive its orders from the Catholic Church through the historic Anglican Communion. The ACC has often been dismissed by the churches of the Anglican Communion for being irregular and illegal, and many will point to the strange events of the so-called Denver Consecrations which marked the beginning of walking apart from the Anglican Communion as a church in its own right, upholding the Catholic Faith.

In Denver in 1978, with the majority of the Episcopal Church in America and the Anglican Church in Canada following their altered doctrine of Christianity, those who sought to remain faithful to the Christianity they had received realised that, in order for the Church to continue, it would be necessary to have Bishops to act as the instruments of unity. To this end, it was agreed that the Rev Charles David Dale Doren would be the first bishop to be consecrated for the new church which was to be named the Anglican Church in North America. Shortly after, this church split up along the party lines that it had inherited from the Episcopal Church. One of the bodies became the Anglican Catholic Church, and it derives a significant strand of its orders from these Denver Consecrations.

It was agreed that Bishop Doren would be consecrated by the retired Bishop of Springfield, the Rt Rev Albert Chambers along with the Rt Rev Francisco de Jesus Pagtakhan of the Philippine Independent Catholic Church, the Rt Rev Mark Pae of Taejon, Korea, and the Rt Rev Charles Boynton, sometime bishop of Puerto Rico. Things did not run smoothly.

Just before the consecration, both Bishop Pae and Bishop Boynton pulled out, the latter suffering from a bout of ill health. However they both sent letters of consent and desire that the consecration be carried out regardless. Although it is alleged that

---

[292] Much of the historical detail about the origins of the Anglican Catholic Church may be found in the "About Us" section on the Provincial Website anglicancatholic.org. An outsider's (and not entirely sympathetic) view of the history of the Continuing Anglican Movement is (Bess, 2006)

they were not truly consensual, the fact of the matter is that Bishop Pae was involved in later consecrations of Anglican Catholic Bishops Willars and Connors, and that Bishop Boynton actually joined the ACC in 1990. Their consent and desire for the consecration of Bishop Doren is therefore visibly demonstrated.

This means, however, that the consecration of Bishop Doren went ahead with only two consecrating bishops physically present instead of the three required by Canon Law. The First Council of Nicaea states,

> It is by all means proper that a bishop should be appointed by all the bishops in the province; but should this be difficult, either on account of urgent necessity or because of distance, three at least should meet together, and the suffrages of the absent [bishops] also being given and communicated in writing, then the ordination should take place. But in every province the ratification of what is done should be left to the Metropolitan.[293]

Here is explicit sanction of bishops sending their consent via letter but it does seem, *prima facie*, that two bishops is insufficient for a valid consecration. Yet, digging a little deeper, the first Apostolic Canon states, "A bishop is to be ordained by two or three bishops."[294]

Of course, the standard has become that three bishops should ordinarily participate in the consecration of a bishop and, after Bishop Doren, all Anglican Catholic bishops have been consecrated with at least three consecrators and often many more. Nonetheless, it is highly likely that there have been bishops in the wider Catholic Church who were consecrated by two rather than three others and whose validity has not been questioned.

Further, and this is pertinent to the English Church, St Bede the Venerable publishes correspondence between Pope St Gregory and St Augustine of Canterbury who was responsible for restructuring the Church in England.

> St Augustine asks – may a bishop be ordained without other bishops being present, in case there be so great a distance between them, that they cannot easily come together?
>
> Pope St Gregory answers – As for the church of England, in which you are as yet the only bishop, you can no otherwise ordain a bishop than in the absence of other bishops; unless

---

[293] First Council of Nicæa, Canon IV
[294] Apostolic Canons, (FEF II, ¶1237 p 130)

> some bishops should come over from Gaul, that they may be present as witnesses to you in ordaining a bishop. But we would have you, my brother, to ordain bishops in such a manner, that the said bishops may not be far asunder, that when a new bishop is to be ordained, there be no difficulty, but that other bishops, and pastors also, whose presence is necessary, may easily come together. Thus, when, by the help of God, bishops shall be so constituted in places everywhere near to one another, no ordination of a bishop is to be performed without assembling three or four bishops. For, even in spiritual affairs, we may take example by the temporal, that they may be wisely and discreetly conducted. It is certain, that when marriages are celebrated in the world, some married persons are assembled, that those who went before in the way of matrimony, may also partake in the joy of the succeeding couple. Why, then, at this spiritual ordination, wherein, by means of the sacred ministry, man is joined to God, should not such persons be assembled, as may either rejoice in the advancement of the new bishop, or jointly pour forth their prayers to Almighty God for his preservation?[295]

The teaching here is that only one bishop is needed for the consecration of another to be valid; the others serve as witnesses to the fact and represent the consent of the Catholic Church. Pope Gregory is clear in setting out that, in grave cases of absences of Catholic bishops, a bishop consecrated by fewer than three bishops is truly a Catholic bishop. This does not throw into doubt the validity of the consecrations, but rather their regularity. It may also be that the consecrations of Bishops in the Church of England are just as "irregular" as the Chambers' succession.

What does regularity mean in this context? By its very etymology, regularity demonstrates the rule by which the bishops live. Many of the modern phenomenon of *episcopi vagantes* are regular only to themselves and their interpretation of whatever rules, canons, and polity they choose. Bishop Doren was indeed validly consecrated, however he was not regularly consecrated within the regularity defined by the Episcopal Church. Bishop John Howe, the Secretary General of the Anglican Consultative Council declared that the ordinations were invalid because they did not have the sanction of the whole church. Bishop Chambers was also asked to leave ECUSA.[296]

---

[295] (Bede, 1999) I, xxvii, p 45-46
[296] "Episcopal Bishop Asked to Quit for Consecration Role" Washington Post, April 7th 1978

Although it was unfortunate to have only two consecrators present at Bishop Doren's consecration, it did not affect its validity, but the consent that it received showed the strength of the intention of Bishop Doren and subsequently consecrated Bishops. The fact that the Chambers Succession flourished into a jurisdiction with a clear constitution, a clear purpose, and a clear desire to preserve the Catholic Faith, means that it cannot be compared with little groups of *episcopi vagantes*. Bishop Howe's comments about the "whole church" not consenting to the consecration would invalidate his own episcopacy as the whole Roman Catholic Church, especially the Pope, did not consent to the consecration of Archbishop Parker and his confraternity following the schism from Rome.

Further, the fact that bishops considered regular in the Anglican Communion have joined the ACC and participated in episcopal consecrations lends strength to the fact that those orders are valid. The current Bishop of the Diocese of the United Kingdom, the Rt Rev Damien Mead, was consecrated in 2008. His chief consecrator, the Rt Rev Rommie Starks, had himself had a former Church of England bishop as a consecrator, namely the Rt Rev Br John-Charles Vockler.[297]

This history of the Continuing Anglican movement demonstrates that although there are certain "irregularities" in the succession of the ACC, they are neither clandestine, nor deliberately lawless but rather they arose just once in response to changes in Catholic doctrine in the Episcopal Church and subsequently the Church of England. Thus, the ACC derives its orders through the historic Church of England. Given the factual invalidity of *Apostolicae Curae* and the involvement of those with undoubted Catholic orders in the consecrations of Bishops Chambers, Pagtakhan, Pae and Boynton and, further, Cranmer, Latimer, Ridley and all other bishops in 1534, it is clear that a Bishop possessing Catholic orders must also possess valid orders in the Anglican system regardless of their personal theology.

Thus, the ACC does have a claim to receiving its orders from the Catholic Church through the Anglican Communion as well as from the Old Catholic lineages, most notably the Polish National Catholic Church whose orders are recognised by Rome. Perhaps this is fitting to have lineages from the Church of England and the Roman Catholic Church converge in the ACC.

---

[297] Bishop Vockler (1924 – 2014) was Bishop of Adelaide (1959 – 1963) and then Polynesia (1963 – 1968) but was also an Assistant Bishop in the Church of England Dioceses of Chelmsford (1972 – 1974) and Southwark (1974 – 1975). He joined the Anglican Catholic Church in 1994 and eventually became the Metropolitan Archbishop (2001 – 2005) before he retired to Australia.

Anglicanism ad fontem

One "family resemblance" to Anglicanism has been demonstrated in the Apostolic Succession of bishops. However, the method previously employed of examining words from their original or earliest recorded meanings has not yet been employed and it ought to yield further points of reference for Wittgenstein's technique.

It is of note that the Venerable St Bede, in writing his Ecclesiastical History of the English Church, uses the Latin title *Historiam Ecclesiasticam Gentis Anglorum*. Of course, it must be recognised that the Angles did not reach the British Isles until the Fifth and Sixth Centuries with St Bede himself writing in the Eighth Century. Thus it was indeed the Angles[298] who encountered St Augustine of Canterbury in AD597. St Bede's history stretches back before this, mentioning St Alban and King Lucius. The adjective "Anglican", according to Avis,[299] is found in letters between St Thomas Beckett and John of Salisbury in referring to the *ecclesia Anglicana*. The Magna Carta contains the immortal declaration that *"Anglicana ecclesia libera sit"* indicating that the Church of England would be free from the control of the king and the barons and thus stand separately from the secular feudal system. As Avis points out, the Reformers use the same phrase to mean exactly the opposite. This would indicate strongly that there is a sense in which Anglicanism might pre-date the Reformation and that threads of this would pass through into what has become the Church of England today.

Culture has a vast impact on how Christianity is expressed. We can see this quite clearly in the Early Church with the great schools of Antioch and Alexandria each putting forward nuances and balances on the Church as a whole. In that sense, they have been more influential on expressing Christian Doctrine in the Early Church than Rome. In reviewing the Seven Oecumenical Councils, Stephen Need points out[300] how the different ways of thinking in Antioch and Alexandria have produced heresies and addressed those heresies before the great Councils assembled. According to Need, Antioch focusses on "the unity of God; the humanity of Jesus; the distinction between the two natures of Christ; and the 'plain-sense' rather than the allegorical interpretation of scripture." This is contrasted with the school of Alexandria which had an "interest in philosophy rather than rhetoric; it was other-worldly rather than this-worldly; it tended to concentrate on the divinity of Christ and to speak of the incarnation in terms of the unity rather than the distinctions between the divinity and the humanity; it was thoroughly Platonist in its

---

[298] *Sed Angeli?*
[299] (Sykes, et al., 1988) p 460
[300] (Need, 2008) p 17 – 39

philosophical outlook, emphasising the divinity of the Logos or Son; it developed an allegorical method of interpreting Scripture."

Even today, the Orthodox Church presents itself to the world in terms of ethnicity and autocephalous jurisdictions all in communion with one another – the Greek Orthodox Church, the Russian Orthodox Church, the Romanian Orthodox Church, et al. It can be seen, then, how different cultural appreciations of the Christian Faith express their orthodoxy within their rites and ceremonies and yet remain committed to that orthodoxy by holding to the same councils. It seems reasonable, then, to understand Anglicanism in an ethnic and historical context from which expressions of theology are revealed.

The periods of reformation in England are unique in the sixteenth century. The catalyst for reformation is essentially politically motivated in Henry VIII but, as history shows, there are so many strands affecting how the Church of England developed. The 1549 Book of Common Prayer is deliberately created to ease the country into Protestant theology and, even with revisions in 1552 and 1559, is never sufficiently Reformed for the Puritans. Catholic composers such as Thomas Tallis and William Byrd are tolerated largely by Elizabeth I whose Protestantism was largely ornate and colourful in opposition to the austere apophacy of the Puritan.

Further, Bruce Kaye[301] argues for this very idea of culture informing the expression of Christianity using the examples of St Bede seeking to demonstrate the need for an understanding of history to King Ceolwulf, of King Alfred learning Latin in order to translate Scripture and the words of the Church Fathers for his people, Archbishop Lanfranc seeking continuity with the English Church across the Norman Invasion and Sir John Fortescue defending an institutional past.

It is this Pre-Reformation "Anglicanism" that generates the different "family resemblances" that may be used to give an idea of what Anglicanism is and how the ACC shares that identity and to what extent. Certainly the historical heritage is shared, especially for the Anglican Catholic Diocese of the United Kingdom and also the Dioceses in the United States, though the latter rely on an Anglican heritage that has arrived through the Scottish Episcopal Church in order to reach the New World.

The Book of Common Prayer

The Book of Common Prayer is central to the expression of worship within the ACC. Given its shared heritage with the historical Catholic Church in England, i.e. the same Church that produced St Bede, St Alcuin, St Alban, St Dunstan and the like,

---

[301] Bruce Kaye, 'Anglicanism' before the Reformation, (Chapman, et al., 2015) p 21 – 33

the ACC therefore regards it as vitally important to worship in a way that encompasses as much of English Catholicism as is possible and is as recognisably so as possible. The goal is try to be both locally English and yet proclaim membership of a larger Church that transcends local boundaries. For Anglican Catholics, *lex orandi lex credendi* is a vital rule by which worship and belief are to be examined.

The ACC deliberately subscribes to Anglican Liturgy and, being Catholic, seeks to contend for the faith which was once delivered unto the saints. The Liturgy must reflect this and so the traditional Liturgy is something to be preserved in the Book of Common Prayer as noted above in Cranmer's intentions. One of the uniquely Anglican characteristics is its ability to balance corporate worship and individual worship. Both the individual and the body are important in Christian thought: this may be seen in the model of perfection, namely the Godhead in which the Three persons are each distinct and yet each fully the One God. This is the inspiration behind the Book of Common Prayer. Again, the key word is "common": it is a liturgy that the congregation shares with the Church. It is designed specifically for all members of the Church to use.

Given the Protestant influences in the history of the Church of England, there are questions to answer about the Book of Common Prayer. Further, given the history of the Book, its revisions and reasons for those revisions, can Anglican Catholics be sure that they are being true to *lex orandi, lex credendi* and the Catholic Church, especially before the English language was recognisable?

Within the history of the Anglican Church, there are peculiarly English ways of doing the Roman Rite. The most important of these is the Sarum Rite which formed the basis of the Reformed Liturgy of the Anglican Church in the 1549 Book of Common Prayer. The major casualty of this is the movement away from the Canon of the Mass of the 1549 Prayer Book to the severely truncated version of the 1559 and subsequent Prayer Books. The later Books of Common Prayer end abruptly with the words of consecration and this causes difficulty when trying to hold to the traditional shape of the Liturgy.

The Anglo-Catholic solution is to utilise the fact that the Prayer Books are based on the Sarum Use which is itself a version of the Roman Rite. This meant that they can keep the substance of the rite with the lessons and collects and many of the prayers and use the Gregorian Canon or the Canon of the 1549 Prayer Book without damaging the shape or sense of the Liturgy. This concordance has allowed a truly Anglican rite to be used with great effect and is found in the Anglican and the English Missals. In the use of these missals, the ACC is using a rite which is recognisable to the Roman Latin Rite (if not identical) in the language of its indigenous culture. Anglican Catholics can be assured that, when they go to Mass, they are using a liturgy that has its roots back to the first liturgies, preserves the sense of the original language and allows them to worship God in their own culture.

The ACC has made its position on its standards of worship clear:

> The Book of Common Prayer in its 1549 English, 1928 American, 1954 South African, and 1962 Canadian editions, and the 1963 edition of the Church of India, Pakistan, Burma, and Ceylon as well as The Supplement To The Book of Common Prayer (C.I.P.B.C.) of 1960 shall be the Standard of Public Worship of this Church, together with The Anglican Missal, The American Missal, The English Missal, and other missals and devotional manuals, based on and conforming to those editions of The Book of Common Prayer.[302]

Having read the Anglican Catholic declaration of the Standard of Worship, it is natural to wonder why, if the Book of Common Prayer is to be truly unifying by being common, so many variations are permitted. Indeed, some Anglican Catholic clergy will use the Anglican Breviary or the Monastic Diurnal instead of the Book of Common Prayer for their daily prayers mandated by canon. Why, if the Book of Common Prayer has an order for the Celebration of the Mass, does it permit the use of Missals?

For those who attended the Congress of St Louis, a fight for the 1928 Book of Common Prayer was a fight for the 1549 Book of Common Prayer read through four hundred years of history, one hundred and fifty of them as part of a country independent from British Rule. This is what the Anglican Catholic Constitution means when it requires liturgical texts to be conformed to the 1549 Book of Common Prayer: the revisions made throughout history have sought out the Catholic Faith as expressed through its Anglican Heritage. Other countries, however, have their own history distinct from the Catholic Church in the United States and, consequently, their own Books of Common Prayer as a result. Not all will do, but those that do conform to the Catholic Faith are certainly permitted.

It is certainly justifiable to ask why, given the centrality to liturgical worship of the Book of Common Prayer, the use of missals and breviaries be allowed. Here, the Anglican Missal makes its apology.

> Loyalty to the Prayer Book has become a battle cry. As such it is used to confound one's enemies, and hence does not always

---

[302] Constitution of the Anglican Catholic Church, Article XIV

become a principle of personal practice or intelligent action on the part of those who proclaim it.

Loyalty to the Prayer Book implies knowledge and sympathetic understanding of our liturgy. For the Prayer Book is the result of long evolution in worship, and that evolution still continues. When liturgy ceases to develop, as with any other living thing, it is dying or dead. "Stick to the Prayer-Book" may be good advice. But those who give it are often those who do not realize that Prayer-Book offices cannot – simply cannot be celebrated if one sticks to the Prayer Book in the sense of doing no more than what is therein ordered. Are there to be no vestments? Not even the surplice and stole is ordered.

Cross and candles? There is no Prayer-Book authority for them. Of ceremonial customs there is little. Vested choirs, processions, processional crosses, flags and banners and many other things dear to the heart of the "Prayer Book Churchmen," are unmentioned. Hymns are permitted but only one Hymn, *Veni Creator* is given. And so it goes. The use of most of these is the result of following not Prayer-Book directions, but the living Catholic tradition of the Church.

In other words, the Prayer-Book Rite must be treated as an apocopated liturgy, for that is precisely what it is. That is to say, our liturgy cannot be celebrated without addition of material or knowledge which the Prayer-Book fails to supply. And when such supplementary material and the Prayer-Book Eucharistic formularies are published together as one book, the result is called a "Missal". Now it is impossible to publish such a book and please everybody. One person wishes little in the way of such additions. Another wishes much. To be of wide service, such a book should be inclusive rather than exclusive, and those who believe in the guidance of the Holy Spirit of the Church will not doubt that the evolutionary process, which is so characteristic of the Western Liturgy, will surely, if slowly, eliminate that which is unworthy.[303]

Thus a common theme may be readily discerned, namely, the 1549 Book of Common Prayer. Indeed, the Collects, Epistles and Gospels of the 1549 Book of Common Prayer are incorporated in all the others, in the missals and in the breviaries. The

---

[303] Introduction to the Anglican Missal.

same language is used. The psalms are those translated by Coverdale. Inherited from the Elizabethan Settlement is that peculiar Anglican genius of essential unity in peculiar diversity centred on that Catholic Faith which Anglican Catholics have in common with countless Christians both living and departed.

Here it is to be noted that the ACC satisfies some rather crucial criteria of what it is to be Anglican – a valid, Catholic succession of Bishops passing through the Anglican lineage as well as the Roman, a shared heritage with the Church of England before the Reformation and a commitment to the use and spirit of the Book of Common Prayer. The history of the Church of England, however, demonstrates that there is a potential inconsistency that requires some resolution. The facts of the matter are that the Church of England at the Reformation was Protestant, perfectly beneficial practices were done away, the monasteries closed and the official doctrine of the Church changed. If the official doctrine of the Church of England was changed then how can being Anglican be consistent with being Catholic?

Protestantism and Anglicanism

Given that the ACC is not in communion with Rome and claims a shared heritage with the Church of England, is it fair to call it a Protestant Church? Again, the problem of meaning arises. If "Protestant" means any church that shares a heritage with another which broke away from Rome at the Reformation then this would apply to the ACC. The trouble is that the word "Protestant"[304] suffers from the same problem as "Anglican" in being an umbrella term for a multiplicity of churches: in fact, it could be argued that "Anglican" is vaguely defined precisely because of the multiplicity of Protestant churches which the Church of England has sought to embrace within its structure.

Further, care must be taken not to read into terms a cultural usage which arise from the unfortunate consequences of the ways in which churches have grown apart. The word "heretic" has a perfectly good definition as one who holds to a theological opinion outside Catholic Doctrine and yet its usage today is predominantly pejorative. The same is true for "Protestant" which comes from serious invective from polemicists from the Roman Catholic Church in which Protestantism is necessarily regarded as a heresy in its rejection of the Universal Jurisdiction of the Papacy. There is not one single Protestantism, and a mistake that is often made, often quite innocently, is to talk of a single Protestant theology when there are many.

---

[304] So does the word "Reformed" which might mean an ecclesial institution that arises from the Reformation or, more popularly, a particular Protestant theology associated (but not necessarily identical) with that of Calvin.

Some Protestant doctrines may be heretical,[305] some may be *theologumena*:[306] only honest study on clear principles can tell.

Differences between Protestants in England may also be seen in the development of the Church of England which largely regarded itself as Protestant[307] but from which certain Protestants such as the Dissenters who wanted to dissociate Church from State, and other Puritans who wanted alterations to Church ritual and Church government.[308]

It must be said, though, that the ACC does not see itself as a truly Protestant Church. This is not on the grounds of a desire for disunity and dissociation from those who hold to a Protestant theology, or of regarding the term "Protestant" as a pejorative, but rather due to the facts of its belief and their coherence to the same theological principles inherent in the Primitive Church held in common with Roman Catholicism and Orthodoxy to their fullest extent in the Church of the first millennium. Indeed, its adherence to Catholicism as shown above is unlike Protestant groups. Given the importance of the doctrine of the First Millennium, it might be argued that the ACC regards itself as pre-denominational and thus distances itself from the more obvious Protestantism of Calvinism, Zwinglism and Lutheranism. Yet, famously, the Oxford Movement theologians have sought to demonstrate that the Church of England is not properly Protestant.[309] This is understandable, given that some Roman and Orthodox polemicists use "Protestant" as a catch-all term wherewith to avoid further engagement with individual bodies, but it is a controversial position. If the Tractarians are correct then the ACC has nothing to prove because it shares a heritage with the Church of England. If, however, they are incorrect then this calls the ACC's "pre-denominationalism" into question for the same reason. As will be shown, the fact that the Oxford Movement have a view of history that is not shared by many reputable historians like Alister McGrath and Diarmaid MacCullough does not disprove the claim of the ACC – in fact, it strengthens its identity as a Continuing Anglican Church. With regards to differences with other Churches, it might be better to agree with Fr Stephen Damick

---

[305] Such as Spong's rejection of the Resurrection of Our Lord.
[306] Such as the *Primacy* of the Pope as opposed to his Universal Jurisdiction.
[307] This may be seen in the Coronation Oath of 1688 in which the Monarch swears to "maintain in the United Kingdom the Protestant Reformed Religion established by law".
[308] (New, 1964) p2
[309] It may be wondered whether, given the Church of England's "official" Protestantism, the Tractarians' efforts actually rescue the term "Protestant" from the commonly held position that "Protestant" and "Catholic" are mutually exclusive terms.

when he quotes Paul Evdokimov as saying, "We know where the Church is; it is not for us to judge and say where it is not."[310]

The Meaning of being Protestant

Again, it is necessary to return *ad fontem verborum*. The word "Protestant" strictly comes from the Christians who made the Protestation of Speyer in 1529. Specifically, this was a petition raised by six princes and fourteen "Imperial Free Cities" to the Holy Roman Emperor Charles V protesting against his *Reichsacht* (Imperial outlawing) of Martin Luther at the Diet of Worms in 1521. In making this protest, the petitioners were stating clearly their adherence to the principles of the Reformation.[311] Of course, in 1529, the Church of England was very much a part of the Roman Catholic Church and, given Henry VIII's antipathy towards Martin Luther, it can be seen that England would have been very much on the side of Charles V at the Diet of Speyer if it had been involved at all. In that original sense, the Church of England, and thus Anglicanism, cannot be seen to be Protestant. If neither Henry VIII nor his ambassadors were at Speyer then how could they protest?

Of course, that is not good enough an argument to demonstrate that the Church of England is not Protestant. For, if after the Reformation, Anglicanism accepts elements of the theology of the Lutherans, Calvinists and Zwinglians, which are assuredly *theologically* Protestant, then it must, too, be *theologically* Protestant at least at the official level and top-down.

The "Protestant principle"[312] has popularly said to consist of the Five *Solae*: *Sola Fide*, *Sola Scriptura*, *Sola Gratia*, *Solo Christo*, and *Soli Deo gloria* and these are meant to contrast with Roman Catholic doctrine. These *solae* are said to have Patristic support and yet, the Orthodox Churches also have patristic support for their understanding of the Catholic Faith which is markedly different from the Western approach – Roman or Protestant. Further, the Five *Solae* are not cited as definitively Protestant principles at the time of the Reformation. Indeed, in 1916, Theodore Engelder can only speak about *sola scriptura*, *sola gratia*, and *sola fide*.[313] Protestant theologies are much more complex than the slogans of "*sola!*" and often it is difficult to pin down the exact departure from Catholicism, especially following appeals from all sides to St Augustine of Hippo. This makes an important point about *theologoumena*, i.e. the sphere of pious opinions where definitive statements

---

[310] (Damick, 2011) p41
[311] See, for example (McGrath, 2001) p 62
[312] If, indeed, it can be said that there is a single Protestant principle!
[313] Theodore Engelder, "The Three Principles of the Reformation: sola scriptura, sola gratia, and sola fide" in Four Hundred Years: Commemorative Essays on the Reformation of Dr Martin Luther and Its Blessed Results, p 97.

of doctrine and dogma are absent. It is the regarding of statements *theologoumena* which were hitherto mandated by Papal decree that made the Elizabethan Settlement possible.

Nonetheless, a definition of Protestant may be made. If the Lutherans and Reformed theologians, such as Luther, Calvin, Zwingli, Melancthon, Bucer et al are regarded as Protestant, then any follower who accepts as dogmatic aspects of their distinctive theologies, their nuances and their developments[314] which are different from the dogmata of Roman Catholicism <u>and</u> the Eastern Orthodox Church must also be Protestant. For the sixteenth century, perhaps the three *solae* are needed to determine Protestantism, especially *sola fide*.

The New Advent Catholic Encyclopedia states in its entry under "Anglicanism":[315]

> The great principles and tenets set forth in the works of Luther, Melanchthon, and Calvin, or Zwingli, are reproduced with or without modifications, but substantially, and often almost verbatim in the literature of the English Reformation. The chief doctrines which are essentially and specifically characteristic of the Protestant Reformation as a whole are the following nine:
> - rejection of the Papacy,
> - denial of the Church Infallibility;
> - Justification by Faith only;
> - supremacy and sufficiency of Scripture as Rule of Faith;
> - the triple Eucharistic tenet [viz. (a) that the Eucharist is a Communion or Sacrament, and not a Mass or Sacrifice, save in the sense of praise or commemoration; (b) the denial of Transubstantiation and worship of the Host; (c) the denial of the sacrificial office of the priesthood and the propitiatory character of the Mass];
> - the non-necessity of auricular Confession;
> - the rejection of the invocation of the Blessed Virgin and the Saints;
> - the rejection of Purgatory and omission of prayers for the dead;
> - the rejection of the doctrine of Indulgences.

---

[314] Especially on questions of authority and soteriology.
[315] https://www.newadvent.org/cathen/01498a.htm (Accessed 22nd February 2021)

> To these may be added three disciplinary characteristics which are founded on doctrine:
> - the giving of Communion in both kinds;
> - the substitution of tables for altars; and
> - the abolition of monastic vows and the celibacy of the clergy.

What is noticeable here is that all of these terms are defined in terms of Roman Catholicism. Neither Ignatian Catholicism nor its obverse in Cyrillic-Vincentian Catholicism are defined in terms of Rome and her Pope. And this is a key point: Catholicism is not the same as Roman Catholicism neither in its Ignatian sense, nor in its Vincentian sense. If it were then the Orthodox Churches would, in their claim to adhere to the same body of doctrine, recognise the Papal claims, receive the *filioque*, and the Roman doctrine of Purgatory. Indeed, looking at the criteria for Protestantism above, some of the statements would apply to the Orthodox Church.

Protestantism in all its forms is therefore something that exists not necessarily in opposition to Catholicism but rather as an exclusively Western opposition to the supreme authority of the Pope. This does raise some issues: a body extricating from a long-established authority has to seek a new identity. For the continental Reformers, this identity is bound up in the leading theologians such as Luther, Calvin and Zwingli. Already, there is marked difference for Anglicanism is not called Cranmerism nor Edwardianism et c. There are aspects of these continental Reformers that are decidedly non-Catholic: for example, the bare Memorialism (falsely) attributed to Zwingli and yet embraced by many today, or the push for lay-presidency at the Eucharist in the Anglican Church in Sydney, Australia.

How is Anglicanism Protestant?

In rejecting the Papal claims, Anglicanism has set itself up as an intentionally Protestant theology. As political leaders enter and exit the stage in the formation of the Church of England, thus the influence of the continental reformers jostles in the minds of Convocation, Parliament and Crown.

H. A. Hodges makes a simple logical point about the Church of England.

> If, then, the Anglican Reformation was an attempt to recover the faith of the undivided Church, is not that equivalent to saying that it was an attempt to return to Orthodoxy?[316]

---

[316] (Hodges, 1947) p 12 - 13

It is quite obvious that nowhere in the Book of Common Prayer may be found the Hail Mary, nor any reference to the Mother of God or the Theotokos. Further, the suppression of the intercession of the saints is completely uncharacteristic of the Orthodox Church. The great ikonoclasm of English Churches which were stripped of all imagery and whitewashed shows an institutional rejection of the Seventh Oecumenical Council. With Hodges, it can be said that if there was a Reformation in England, then it was certainly neither Roman Catholic, nor Orthodox.

It has, however, been established that Anglican Orders are far from null and void in the Catholic sense. Further, it has also been established that the Book of Common Prayer is at least patient of the Real Presence. What has been rejected is the Tridentine definition of Transubstantiation which is dependent on Aristotelian philosophy and is also rejected by the Orthodox Church. Hooker does not reject the Real Presence but prefers an "agnostic" approach.[317] Both Bishop Gheast and Queen Elizabeth I object to Article XXIX which states that the wicked receive not the Body and Blood of Christ in the Eucharist demonstrating that belief in the objective presence of Christ in the elements is still prevalent in the middle of the sixteenth century. Thus, if the historic episcopate has been preserved and the body and blood of Christ being distributed to the faithful baptised, then there is a strong claim that the Church of England remained Catholic at the Reformation in the Ignatian sense.

This leaves a problem of Cyrillic-Vincentian Catholicism. True Catholic doctrine has been lost in the Reformation – the intercession of the saints, the place of Our Lady, the adoration of Our Lord in the Blessed Sacrament, the acceptability of synergism et c. If the Church of England rejects Catholic doctrine at the Reformation, then it cannot be Catholic in the Cyrillic-Vincentian sense and thus there must be a problem with the Ignatian Catholicism it claims.

In addressing this issue, it may be seen that there is a commitment within the Church of England government to the faith of the Primitive Church. The Canons of 1571 state of preachers that "especially shall they see to it that they teach nothing in the way of a sermon, which they would have religiously held and believed by the people, save what is agreeable to the teaching of the Old or New Testament, and what the Catholic fathers and ancient bishops have collected from this selfsame doctrine."[318] Further, as stated above, the Book of Common Prayer appeals to the Primitive Church for its authority.

---

[317] William Crockett, Holy Communion (Sykes, et al., 1988) p308 - 321
[318] Canon VI of the 1571 Canons of the Church of England.

Bishop John Jewel is clear that the Church of England has some claim on being Catholic.

> Further, if we do show it plainly that God's holy Gospel, the ancient bishops, and the primitive Church do make on our side, and that we have not without just cause left these men, and rather have returned to the Apostles and old Catholic fathers; and if we shall be found to do the same not colourably or craftily, but in good faith before God, truly, honestly, clearly, and plainly; and if they themselves which fly our doctrine, and would be called Catholics, shall manifestly see how all these titles of antiquity, whereof they boast so much, are quite shaken out of their hands; and that there is more pith in this our cause than they thought for; we then hope and trust that none of them will be so negligent and careless of his own salvation, but he will at length study and bethink himself to whether part he were best to join him. Undoubtedly, except one will altogether harden his heart and refuse to hear, he shall not repent him to give good heed to this our Defence, and to mark well what we say, and how truly and justly it agreeth with Christian religion.[319]

The reformed Church of England maintained the principle of appealing to the Early Church. The preface to the 1662 Book of Common Prayer states:

> In which review we have endeavoured to observe the like moderation, as we find to have been used in the like case in former times. And therefore of the sundry Alterations proposed unto us, we have rejected all such as were either of dangerous consequence (as secretly striking at some established Doctrine, or laudable Practice of the Church of England, or indeed of the whole Catholick Church of Christ) or else of no consequence at all, but utterly frivolous and vain.

Thus any alteration to the faith and worship of the Church of the England must pass the criterion of the Vincentian Canon.

Of course, there is an issue here. "The way of sinners is made plain with stones, but at the end thereof is the pit of hell"[320] or, in more popular phrasing, "the pathway to

---

[319] John Jewel, The Apology of the Church of England, Part I. http://anglicanhistory.org/jewel/apology/01.html (Accessed 22nd February 2021)
[320] Ecclesiasticus xxi.10

Hell is paved with good intentions." Here are only intentions to follow the doctrine of the Primitive Church and yet there are clear rejections of the doctrine of the Primitive Church apparent within the reformed Church of England. These may be clearly seen in the Formularies – the Book of Common Prayer, the Homilies and the XXXIX Articles. Of course, together with the Roman Catholic Church and the Orthodox Church, the ACC regards the Primitive Church as being that which possesses and follows the Seven Oecumenical Councils, though this admittedly does rather present an ambiguity with regard to the period AD787-1054. It is this intersection of Eastern and Western Christianity that ensures the Vincentian-Cyrillic Catholicity for the Church and suggests that the theology espoused by just the first four councils is incomplete. Certainly the ACC regards the Primitive Church as existing for longer than the first four councils mentioned in the Ten Articles of 1536.

This said, the Homily against peril of Idolatry quotes the sixth council favourably:

> After Gregories time, Constantine Bishoppe of Rome assembled a councell of Bishoppes in the West Church, and did condemne Philippicus then Emperour, and Iohn Bishoppe of Constantinople of the heresie of the Monothelites, not without a cause in deede, but very iustly.

This suggests that the sixth council, although not as venerable in the eyes of the Ten Articles and the subsequent emergent Anglican theology as the first four, is still regarded as possessing some authority. The same homily nonetheless contains a clear rejection of the seventh council.

This certainly implies a different theology from the Primitive Church which, through the use of ikons and veneration of saints, has a more affirmative view of humanity through the Doctrine of the Incarnation than that of those who would see images and veneration removed. If Our Lord is truly human, then He can be depicted in an image and, like a photograph, His image will inspire worship in the heart of the beholder.[321] If an image of Our Lord must not inspire such worship then there is some disconnect between Our Lord's physical existence and our own, something that impairs our humanity from being His. The difference between Christ and Man, it might be said, is sin but this is not a physical characteristic. This might suggest that a major issue underlying the rejection of the seventh council lies with how sin affects humanity – an issue that is central to the reason for the Reformation.

---

[321] See the argument used by St John Damascene, *Exact Exposition of the Orthodox Faith*, XVI p 88 (NPNF IX)

The Protestant Book of Common Prayer?

One of the factors that brought about the Continuing Anglican movement in the first place was an enforced change in liturgy. The United States Prayer Book of 1928 was to be replaced with the 1979 Prayer Book with the use of the former to be discouraged strongly. Thus, with the separation of ECUSA from the Catholic Church in 1977, it became of vital importance to the new Continuing Anglican churches in the United States to hold on to the Prayer Book for which they had fought dearly. But why was it so important? The 1928 Prayer Book was a revision of the 1789 Book that the newly independent Episcopal Church inherited. That book of 1789 reintroduced parts of the 1549 Canon of the Mass referring to the Sacrifice of the Mass which later books removed. By 1928, further revisions reintroduced prayer for the departed. Essentially, the 1928 Book of Common Prayer resembled more the original 1549 Book of Common Prayer.

The 1979 Book of Common Prayer removed passages from some of the prayers. In seeking to understand the objections being raised at the Congress of St Louis, it is instructive to compare the Prayer of Humble Access between the three versions, the two mentioned above in the discussion on Eucharistic Theology, and that of the 1979 Book of Common Prayer.

> We do not presume to come to this thy Table, O merciful Lord, trusting in our own righteousness, but in thy manifold and great mercies. We are not worthy so much as to gather up the crumbs under thy Table. But thou art the same Lord whose property is always to have mercy. Grant us therefore, gracious Lord, so to eat the flesh of thy dear Son Jesus Christ, and to drink his blood, that we may evermore dwell in him, and he in us. Amen.[322]

To be noted is the near identical imprecations of the 1549 and 1928 books of the direct effect of the sacramental grace of eating the flesh and blood of Christ and how this is made vague and robbed of meaning by the 1979 book. By receiving the Body of Christ, the human body is made to conform to that Body and the soul cleansed by the Blood. This makes it clear that there is a Real Presence which effects something in the dichotomist understanding of the human person. For the 1979, this is played down to ambiguity and the leaning towards Receptionism since it suggests that it is the act of eating and drinking that effects the mutual indwelling with Christ rather than the actual Body of Christ being ingested.

---

[322] Prayer of Humble Access from the Holy Eucharist Rite I of the US 1979 BCP

Of course, this business of revision upon revision shows that it must be asked just how Catholic the Book of Common Prayer really is, especially following its original composition in a very Protestant *milieu* and following its intended purpose of allowing Continental Protestantism to gain a foothold in a country once famed for its devotion to the Catholic cause. Given that Pope Leo XIII saw fit to call into question whether the Anglican Ordination Liturgy is truly Catholic, it seems that there is need to ensure that the Book of Common Prayer is truly a book of Catholic Liturgy, i.e. that the faith that this book promotes in its prayer is the Catholic Faith. In order to make this demonstration, it is necessary to examine the intention of the book and thereby show that it does not contradict the Catholic Faith.

The Preface to the First Book of Common Prayer contains much that will aid this investigation.

> There was never any thing by the wit of man so well devised, or so surely established, which (in continuance of time) hath not been corrupted: as (among other things) it may plainly appear by the common prayers in the Church, commonly called divine service: the first original and ground whereof, if a man would search out by the ancient fathers, he shall find that the same was not ordained, but of a good purpose, and for a great advancement of godliness: For they so ordered the matter, that all the whole Bible (or the greatest part thereof) should be read over once in the year, intending thereby, that the Clergy, and specially such as were Ministers of the congregation, should (by often reading and meditation of God's word) be stirred up to godliness themselves, and be more able also to exhort other by wholesome doctrine, and to confute them that were adversaries to the truth.

Here the Catholic principles are evidently at work. The Book of Common Prayer is intended to look back to the Primitive Church in order to ascertain the common prayers and doctrine "for good purpose and for a great advancement of Godliness." This is a commitment to Holy Tradition. Likewise, in ensuring that all have recourse to Holy Scripture, so that the whole thing is read in a year, there is a clear commitment to the primacy of Holy Scripture. That the Book of Common Prayer seeks to oppose heresy by reasoning from Scripture and Tradition, "to confute them that were adversaries to the truth" shows its commitment to Right Reason.

This is not all. There is a commitment to the Vincentian Canon: it opens the principles of Catholicism up to everyone, not just the clergy, and it shows the commitment to the personal holiness of each member of the Church. In continuing the place of the clergy, it is continuing the Sacramental nature and incorporation of the Church.

> And further, that the people (by daily hearing of Holy Scripture read in the Church) should continually profit more and more in the knowledge of God, and bee the more inflamed with the love of his true religion. But these many years passed this Godly and decent order of the ancient fathers, hath bee so altered, broken, and neglected, by planting in uncertain stories, legends, responds, verses, vain repetitions, commemorations, and synodals, that commonly when any book of the Bible was began: before three or four Chapters were read out, all the rest were unread. And in this sort the book of Isaiah was begun in Advent, and the book of Genesis in Septuagesima: but they were only begun, and never read through. After a like sort were other books of Holy Scripture used. And moreover, whereas St Paul would have such language spoken to the people in the church, as they might understand and have profit by hearing the same; the service in this Church of England (these many years) hath been read in Latin to the people, which they understood not; so that they have heard with their ears only; and their hearts, spirit, and mind, have not been edified thereby. And furthermore, notwithstanding that the ancient fathers had divided the psalms into seven portions, whereof every one was called a nocturn, now of late time a few of them have been daily said (and oft repeated) and the rest utterly omitted. Moreover the number and hardness of the rules called the *pie*, and the manifold changings of the service, was the cause, that to turn the book only was so hard and intricate a matter, that many times, there was more business to find out what should be read, then to read it when it was found out.

In this can be seen the reason why the Reformers believed that the Book of Common Prayer had to be composed. While a monastery could keep the daily offices of prayer and pray and study the Bible as part of their monastic calling, the layfolk had no recourse to Holy Scripture and had never in all likelihood heard it entirely. It was being mumbled and the structure of the old breviary with its verses and responds and the like was turning the whole business of public prayer into "vain repetitions" against which Our Lord warns His Church.[323] With regard to the Religious in the Church who spend their day with the breviary, the ACC knows that they are engaged in wholesome prayer. For the layfolk whose lives are busy bringing Christ into their secular work, however, the Book of Common Prayer provides a staple diet which gives them access to the whole of Scripture without befuddling them with devotions that they simply have no time for in their lives.

There is something additional in evidence here. This preface mentions nocturns. These are parts of the Benedictine Office of Readings prayed in the middle of the night, each nocturn consisting of six psalms and three readings on a ferial day. This, and the desire to have the whole psalter read in public in a month, shows that the Book of Common Prayer is following an older scheme – the Benedictine Rule which, in turn, looks back to older rules and schemas. The Book of Common Prayer opens this rule up to all without a need to become professed monks and nuns. It provides a way for each person to make a commitment to obedience, stability and habitual conversion of the soul to Christ. Since Christians are now profoundly more literate and have greater access to books than their brothers and sisters in the sixteenth century, there is no real problem with the use of missals and breviaries provided that they do conform to the Book of Common Prayer.

> And where heretofore, there hath been great diversity in saying and singing in churches within this realm: some following Salisbury use, some Hereford use, some the use of Bangor, some of York, and some of Lincoln: Now from henceforth, all the whole realm shall have but one use. And if any would judge this way more painful, because that all things must be read upon the book, whereas before, by the reason of so often repetition, they could say many things by heart: if those men will weigh their labour, with the profit in knowledge, which daily they shall obtain by reading upon the book, they will not refuse the pain, in consideration of the great profit that shall ensue thereof.

It may be seen here in the purpose of the Book that uniformity of worship allows for a greater chance for everyone to take to heart the texts mentioned. Until quite recently, many people in the British Isles could still mention phrases from the Book of Common Prayer. People have memorised and loved these texts by their repetition, and as a result have taken comfort in the word of God.

---

[323] St Matthew vi.7

Further, it is worth noting that the various uses mentioned here have been absorbed into the Book. Many of the collects and the like have come from the Salisbury use, i.e. the Sarum rite of the late Middle Ages which itself was drawn from sources such as the Gelasian Sacramentary.

> And for as much as nothing can, almost, be so plainly set forth, but doubts may rise in the use and practising of the same: to appease all such diversity (if any arise), and for the resolution of all doubts, concerning the manner how to understand, do, and execute the things contained in this book: the parties that so doubt, or diversely take any thing, shall alway resort to the Bishop of the Diocese, who by his discretion shall take order for the quieting and appeasing of the same: so that the same order be not contrary to any thing contained in this book.

Again, another Catholic principle is clearly being used, namely that the bishop is seen as the centre of unity. With a liturgy aimed at uniting the people in one common worship, they find themselves united also in the bishop's oversight of the liturgy and its intent.

As to the question of the Sacraments, the 1549 Book of Common Prayer contains a Catholic form to guarantee that the Catholic Sacraments are distributed according to the ancient practices of the Church. There have been revisions in 1552, 1559, and 1662 which have certainly made changes to the services. The 1662 Order for Holy Communion has a canon that is rather short and also possesses the infamous Black Rubric:

> Whereas it is ordained in this Office for the Administration of the Lord's Supper, that the Communicants should receive the same kneeling; (which order is well meant, for a signification of our humble and grateful acknowledgment of the benefits of Christ therein given to all worthy Receivers, and for the avoiding of such profanation and disorder in the holy Communion, as might otherwise ensue;) yet, lest the same kneeling should by any persons, either out of ignorance and infirmity, or out of malice and obstinacy, be misconstrued and depraved: It is hereby declared, That thereby no adoration is intended, or ought to be done, either unto the Sacramental Bread or Wine there bodily received, or unto any Corporal Presence of Christ's natural Flesh and Blood. For the Sacramental Bread and Wine remain still in their very natural substances, and therefore may not be adored; (for that were Idolatry, to be abhorred of all faithful Christians;) and the

> natural Body and Blood of our Saviour Christ are in Heaven, and not here; it being against the truth of Christ's natural Body to be at one time in more places than one.[324]

This was added to the 1552 Prayer Book only days before final printing, over many objections, and sought to assure that kneeling at the Communion did not in any way imply adoration of the host. This sounds very contrary to the committed Anglican Catholic belief in the Real Presence, but it is valuable to compare the Black Rubric above with this:

> Jesus is not there like a piece of meat, not in the realm of what can be measured and quantified...How should we relate to reality? What is "real"?...Concerning the Eucharist it is said to us: The substance is transformed, that is to say, the fundamental basis of its being...Whenever the Body of Christ, that is, the risen and bodily Christ, comes, he is greater than the bread, other, not of the same order. The transformation happens, which affects the gifts we bring by taking them up into a higher order and changes them, even if we cannot measure what happens...The Lord takes possession of the bread and the wine; he lifts them up, as it were, out of the setting of their normal existence into a new order; even if, from a purely physical point of view, they remain the same, they have become profoundly different.[325]

These words were written by the future Pope Benedict XVI and perhaps, as a Tractarian like St John Henry Newman might argue, the Black Rubric can still be read in a Catholic manner. The Christian does not worship any scientifically measurable thing – the Christian worships Christ whose real and objective presence is there but in a way that is inaccessible to wilfully profane scientific methods. The quantum idea that the very act of observation changes matter forces the believer to "draw near with faith" rather than engage in a futile exercise of proving or disproving the existence of God with test tubes and electromagnetic imaging equipment. This drawing near with faith is markedly beneficial since we are justified by faith and thus the act of drawing near to Christ continues the process of justification begun in faith.

It has to be said that this rubric was inserted deliberately by those who wanted to steer the Church in a Protestant direction. While all subsequent Books of Common Prayer admit a fully Catholic reading, following the Catholic Principles has brought the ACC back to the 1549 Book of Common Prayer as its standard of worship and

---

[324] Found at the end of the Order for Holy Communion in the 1552 and 1662 Books of Common Prayer
[325] (Ratzinger, 2003) p 85

those which conform to it – especially the 1928 US Book – together with the use of missals and breviaries without trying to compromise the spirit of the Anglican heritage set out in the preface to the 1549 Book of Common Prayer. Owing to their belief in the Real Presence, Anglican Catholics may, if they wish, perform adoration of the Blessed Sacrament and attend Exposition and Benediction where they are offered.

The 1662 Prayer Book was the standard in the United Kingdom until the Twentieth Century despite having a truncated Eucharistic Prayer and a functional liturgy that was certainly not as rich as it once was. Thus, the Oxford Movement and the Anglo-Catholics often either supplemented the 1662 Eucharistic Prayer with older Eucharistic Prayers such as the Gregorian Canon, or the 1549 Canon. This gave rise to the English and Anglican Missals which have been used more in the U.K. than the U.S. Since both missals are conformed to the 1549 Book of Common Prayer, being in English and using the 1549 Lectionary and Collects, the ACC is able to authorise them for liturgical use.

Therefore, it has been shown that the Book of Common Prayer seeks to be true to Holy Scripture first, Holy Tradition second and Right Reason, third. It has been shown that it is intended to be used by everyone, at all times and in all places. It has been shown that it is based on the same principles for community as Benedictine Spirituality. Further, it has been shown that it provides a Catholic form for the administration of the Sacraments. From this it can be concluded that the 1549 Book of Common Prayer, and the 1928 US Book of Common Prayer from which it is derived, are properly Catholic and a fit liturgy for the Catholic Church.

The Thirty-Nine Articles

Admittedly, the famous Thirty Nine Articles within the Book of Common Prayer do create some division between Anglican Catholics. There are some who regard them as authoritative, and there are those who do not. It is important to understand why they might be seen as authoritative.

One might argue from the Affirmation of St Louis that, because the Book of Common Prayer of 1928 in America and 1962 in Canada are "fully and equally authoritative" and that they contain the Thirty-Nine Articles, the Thirty-Nine Articles must therefore be authoritative in the ACC.

The contrary argument states that the Articles are not the product of doctrine of the Primitive Church. Within the Articles there are clear influences from the Augsberg Confession. In particular, this may be seen in Article XXXV: On the Homilies which states that the Homilies "contain a godly and wholesome Doctrine, and necessary for these times".

Yet the Homilies contain a clear broadside against the teaching of the Seventh Oecumenical Council:

> First, it is alleged by them that maintain images, that all laws, prohibitions, and curses, noted by vs out of the holy Scripture, and sentences of the Doctors also by vs alleged, against images and the worshipping of them, appertain to the idols of the Gentiles or Pagans, as the idol of Jupiter, Mars, Mercury, etc. and not to our images of God, of Christ, and his Saints. But it shall be declared both by God's word, and the sentences of the ancient Doctors, and judgement of the Primitive Church, that all images, as well ours, as the idols of the Gentiles, be forbidden and unlawful, namely in Churches and Temples.[326]

Thus, the Articles could be seen to be doctrinally unreliable and thus not authoritative in the ACC.

These are two arguments for and against requiring the authority of the Articles. Is there a middle ground?

What is apparent from the approach of the Reformers mentioned above is that the traditional Anglican Formularies consistently point outside themselves to the Catholic Principles. These Formularies are not intended to be absolute confessions like those of Augsburg or Westminster.

Thus, the argument for holding the Articles is not all that clear on what it means by "authoritative". The Affirmation of St Louis holds the Book of Common Prayer as authoritative on worship in a liturgical context and not necessarily of doctrine. *Lex orandi, lex credendi,* however, might be called into play here to render the Articles a matter of Catholic Doctrine but we do remember that the Catholic Doctrine must inform liturgy and not the other way round. It is necessary to be careful invoking the Aphorism of Prosper of Aquitaine when dealing with what the Book of Common Prayer contains. The *filioque* is in the Prayer Book and yet is not part of Catholic doctrine of the Primitive Church unless it is read in line with those who believe in the procession of the Holy Ghost from the Father through the Son. In the same way, there are many in the ACC who can indeed reconcile the Articles with the doctrine

---

[326] Homily against Peril of Idolatry, III

of the Primitive Church – indeed, they were designed and written for that very interpretive purpose.

As the ACC bases its doctrine on that of the Primitive Church first and its worship on the Book of Common Prayer and texts conforming to it. This means that where the Articles agree with that doctrine, then they are a restatement of that doctrine, and where they disagree, they are simply wrong. Of course, the good Anglican Catholic will not be too hasty to make that judgement without good and serious study as there is much good doctrine therein. As St Vincent requires, each article must be judged on its own standing within the Catholic Principles.

Hence, the Formularies are, and must be, revised in the light of the Primitive Church as the Church recovers its Catholicism from its time under the influence of the Papacy and the continental reformers. This is not easy when there are Calvinists like Archbishop Whitgift trying to push through (hyper)Calvinist doctrines in the Lambeth Articles of 1595. While the Caroline Divines appeal to the Fathers with great eloquence, their position within the Church of England forces them not to step far beyond the bounds set by the Formularies. With the fear of Roman Catholics infiltrating the establishment, if there is to be any return to the full doctrine of the Catholic Church it must wait until a more favourable time. The beginning of that time occurs when John Keble delivers a sermon on 14th July 1833.

The Catalyst for the Congress

It has been important for the ACC to demonstrate its identity before examining the issues that led to the Congress of St Louis in the first place. One catalyst was the imposition of a new revision of the Book of Common Prayer in the United States: this became the 1979 Book of Common Prayer still in use in ECUSA today. By far, however, the issue that caused the Congress is the matter of the Ordination of Women to Holy Orders.

This is a topic for which space does not permit a full examination of the issue but it is a reflection as to how the Anglican Catholic Church applies the Catholic Principles to show that the Catholic Church has no authority to ordain women to Holy Orders. Clearly, prior to the 1940s, no woman was ordained in the Anglican Communion, thus those who support the issue have the burden of showing that the ordination of women is consonant with the Catholic Principles. Are women seen to be ordained within Holy Scripture, Tradition and Reason?

Looking at Holy Scripture, it is necessary to see women specifically receiving the commission from God and exercising the same sort of ministry as those who are seen to be bishops, priests and deacons. Clearly, as mentioned above, there are no women within the Levitical priesthood. God Himself consecrates the sons of Aaron for the priesthood: The other sons of Levi are to be ministers to the priests.[327] Thus, that the Levitical priesthood is male in character at God's choice. Melchisedek is also male. Our Lord chooses only male disciples and Apostles.[328] At every stage, those set apart for the sacrificial and covenantal ministry at God's ordinance are exclusively male. Is there a reason for it?

While it is not a certainty, the nature of the sacraments makes a good case for why. It is clear from above that the Mass is a participation in the one perfect sacrifice of Christ the Victim offered by Christ the Priest. The priest celebrating the Mass acts *in persona Christi* and is an ikon of Christ. Indeed, this is true of all the sacraments: Our Lord sanctifies the water of baptism by His person; He sanctifies a marriage by His person; He breathes the Holy Ghost on His disciples through His own person. If the priest acts as a conduit of Christ then He does so as an ikon of Christ which is made particular through the grace of his ordination.

St Paul says:

> For a man indeed ought not to cover his head, forasmuch as he is the image and glory of God: but the woman is the glory of the man. For the man is not of the woman; but the woman of the man. Neither was the man created for the woman; but the woman for the man.[329]

And so:

> Thus, while a man is the ikon of God, a woman is the ikon of an ikon of God: both bear the divine image of God but in different ways. Man proceeds physically from Woman and Christ Himself gives this procession a dignity by embracing being born of woman in order to sanctify pregnancy and childbirth. Woman proceeds spiritually from Man because Christ is involved in the Creation of humanity, thus giving a dignity to the ability of man to offer sacrifice to God. A man is a direct ikon of Christ and a woman is a direct ikon of Mary

---

[327] Numbers iii.6
[328] Of course, St Mary Magdalene is regarded as the Apostle to the Apostles which very much cements the supreme value of women in the Church as witnesses to the Resurrection of Our Lord. Like the Blessed Virgin, she is a fundamental witness to the reality of the Incarnation of the Lord. After this, she fades from the view of Church History and her whereabouts have become the stuff of legend on which the likes of Dan Brown capitalise. Unlike the Apostles, she does not have appeared to have engaged in missionary work. St Gregory of Tours (On Miracles, I, xxx) suggests that she went to Ephesus with Our Lady and died there.
[329] I Corinthians xi.7-9

> from whom Christ takes humanity and is thus an indirect ikon of Christ. Man is good because God declares him so. Woman is good because she is the glory of Man and Man is good.[330]

In looking at a picture of a man, no matter the appearance of that man, it is conceivably possible that we could be looking at Christ. It is not possible to say the same thing of a picture of a women. The best that could be said is that that woman could conceivably be Our Lady and thus see the possibility of the infant Christ in her arms nonetheless bearing her genetics.

Thus, there are good grounds for believing based on the doctrine of the Real Presence and the efficacy of the sacraments why the priesthood is male in character. Now, those who support the priesthood of women must do the same. They must show the Church's approval of the ordination of women by the time of the Great Schism. As the late Fr Geoffrey Kirk shows, the majority of arguments in favour of the ordination of women are arguments from silence and have no clear basis in fact.[331]

Thus, to admit the ordination of women means a rejection of the Catholic Sacraments and an impairment of Communion, breaking the very heart of Ignatian Catholicism. The argument made above that rejecting interchangeability of minister is a rejection of communion is why the Continuing Anglican Movement had no choice whatsoever in leaving the Anglican Communion on the grounds that, in accepting communion with ordained women, it was condoning heresy.

What does the ACC continue?

The idea that the Anglican Formularies are malleable under the influence of Scripture, Tradition and Reason puts the ACC firmly in the same school of thought as the Tractarians who rise to the challenge set by Keble in his Assize Sermon. In his conclusion to the famous Tract XC, St John Henry Newman writes:

> Whatever be the authority of the [Declaration] prefixed to the Articles, so far as it has any weight at all, it sanctions the mode of interpreting them above given. For its enjoining the "literal and grammatical sense," relieves us from the necessity of making the known opinions of their framers, a comment upon their text; and its forbidding any person to "affix any new sense to any Article," was promulgated at a time when the

---

[330] (Munn, 2019) p 241
[331] (Kirk, 2016)

> leading men of our Church were especially noted for those Catholic views which have been here advocated.[332]

This tract caused controversy precisely because it hit at the fundamental understanding of Anglicanism at the time. The Articles were meant to be understood in their "plain and literal sense"[333] and, for many Anglicans particularly the Evangelicals, to demonstrate that the Articles could be brought in line with the Council of Trent was tantamount to undoing the Reformation. The polemicist Walter Walsh describes the Oxford Movement as a group of "men who work in the dark to destroy the Protestantism of the Church and Nation."[334]

The Oxford Movement was intended as a means of recovering the historic faith in the light of Parliament's involvement with the Church of Ireland. It was St John Henry Newman who declared that the Oxford Movement began at the Assize Sermon in 1833 given by John Keble.[335] This sermon against National Apostasy was directed against the suppression of ten bishoprics in the Church of Ireland by the Whig government and Keble was unequivocal in his condemnation of the interference by Parliament into the affairs of the Church.

> Should it ever happen (which God avert, but we cannot shut our eyes to the danger) that the Apostolical Church should be forsaken, degraded, nay trampled on and despoiled by the State and people of England, I cannot conceive a kinder wish for her, on the part of her most affectionate and dutiful children, than that she may, consistently, act in the spirit of this most noble sentence ; nor a course of conduct more likely to be blessed by a restoration to more than her former efficiency. In speaking of the Church, I mean, of course, the laity, as well as the clergy in their three orders,– the whole body of Christians united, according to the will of Jesus Christ, under the Successors of the Apostles. It may, by God's blessing, be of some use, to show how, in the case supposed, the example of Samuel might guide her collectively, and each of her children individually, down even to minute details of duty.

---

[332] St John Henry Newman, Tracts for the Times, Number 90, Remarks On Certain Passages In The Thirty-Nine Articles
[333] C.f the preface to the Articles in the 1662 Book of Common Prayer
[334] Walter Walsh The Secret History of the Oxford Movement (5th ed.) (1899). London Church Association. p ix
[335] (Newman, 1993) p112

In mentioning the "Successors of the Apostles", Keble began the scrutiny into the ancient Church which was to break the appearance that the Church began in the sixteenth century.

Thus the Oxford Movement was intended as a conservative anchor for the Church against Erastianism and once more pitted Henry VIII, Edward IV and Elizabeth I against Popes Clement VII, Paul III and Pius V. Its lack of immediate success in the 1840s resulted in convincing several prominent members of the Movement to convert to Roman Catholicism. It is unfortunate that there was then, and still now, the highly disputed view that Roman Catholicism is the One True Catholicism. This is not true for Dr Edward Bouverie Pusey. His biographer, Dr Henry Liddon writes:

> But more especially do the Fathers attest the existence of Catholic agreement in a great body of truth in days when the Church of Christ was still visibly one, and still spoke one language; and thus they also bear witness against the fundamentally erroneous assumptions of modern times, that truth is only that which each man troweth, and that the divisions of Christendom are unavoidable and without remedy.[336]

For Dr Pusey, it is the Catholicism inherent within Anglicanism that must be drawn out following the schisms of the Reformation and that between the Eastern and Western Church:

> It is too likely that all our privileges are impaired by these rents, that the stream of grace no longer runs so richly through all the branches, which are thus torn, though not wholly severed. We have all the more reason to pray for the peace and unity of the Church, as suffering ourselves from its disunion. As we are not saved by ourselves, are not members of our Lord by ourselves, but in His Church and Communion of Saints, so our privileges and the helps to our salvation are, in a mysterious way, wrapped up in the well-being of the Church.[337]

Here may be seen the same desire and intention of the ACC to strengthen the third "branch" of the Catholic Church which has been damaged by the Reformation with the introduction of methods[338] and doctrines[339] contrary to the Catholic Principles.

---

[336] Henry Liddon, DD, Life of Edward Bouverie Pusey, vol I, Chapter XVIII
[337] E. B. Pusey, Parochial Sermons, III, p 241 – 242, 252 – 253 as cited in (Rowell, 1983) p 86
[338] E.g. extreme *Sola Scriptura*.
[339] E.g. "once saved, always saved"

Dr Pusey's "rents" have not been allowed to heal. In 1845, the Oxford Movement effectively ended with Newman's secession to Rome following the unfavourable reception of Tract XC,[340] yet its followers became the first Anglo-Catholics. The 1840s saw the establishment of Anglican religious orders such as the Sisterhood of the Holy Cross,[341] and later in 1865 the Cowley Fathers under Fr R. M. Benson.[342] Fr Charles Lowder pioneered mission work and influenced many clergymen to see themselves as having "supernatural power".[343]

With Newman now a Roman Catholic, it is easy to see why there is a fear that Anglo-Catholicism might lead to Roman Catholicism, especially with priests such as William George Ward writing the Ideal of a Christian Church claiming that submission to Rome was only way that the Church of England could avoid the interference of the State.

> For my own part, I think it would not be right to conceal, indeed I am anxious openly to express, my own most firm and undoubting conviction, that were we, as a Church, to pursue such a line of conduct as has been here sketched, in proportion as we did so, we should be taught from above to discern and appreciate the plain marks of Divine wisdom and authority in the Roman Church, to repent in sorrow and bitterness of heart our great sin in deserting her communion, and to sue humbly at her feet for pardon and restoration.[344]

More Anglo-Catholics converted to Roman Catholicism following the outcome of the Gorham case in 1850 in which a secular court was used to decide on a matter of Anglican Doctrine.[345] Rome has always been seen as the only alternative for those who reject the social and political influences into matters of doctrine, faith and practice.[346] Even as Tractarianism developed into Anglo-Catholicism and Ritualism, it has been attacked by Evangelicals, such as John Kensit and his "Kensitites" who disrupted Anglo-Catholic Masses,[347] and others who brought legal actions against

---

[340] (Chandler, 2003) p51ff
[341] (Pickering, 1989) p130
[342] (Pickering, 1989) p74
[343] (Pickering, 1989) p73
[344] W. G. Ward, The Ideal of a Christian Church, Baxter, 1844 p 473
[345] The Gorham case and the Rev. G. A. Denison. HC Deb 18 March 1850, vol 109 cc1054-6
[346] The founding of the Anglican Ordinariate in 2011 is evidence that this is still the case.
[347] Such as carrying off a statue of the Blessed Virgin Mary from St Matthew's Church, Sheffield on 22nd January 1912. Kensit himself, leader of the Kensitites met his end in October 1902 after being struck by a chisel thrown by a protesting (protestant?!) Anglo-Catholic labourer. The labourer was acquitted. (Cheltenham Chronicle, 13th December 1902)

their priests such as Fr Tooth, Fr Mackonochie and even Bishop Edward King[348] for Catholic practices.

Even as Anglo-Catholicism grew in respectability peaking in the great Anglo-Catholic Congresses of the 1930s, even then it was still very much at odds with the more Protestant voices.[349] The Elizabethan Settlement was beginning to fracture, to which the very existence of the ACC bears witness.

The ACC exists because, in 1976, the Episcopal Church of the United States in which Resolution B-005 was passed:

> "The provisions of these canons for the admission of Candidates, and for the Ordination to the three Orders: Bishops, Priests and Deacons shall be equally applicable to men and women."

At this moment, Catholic Doctrine was changed by a ballot in a Convention that could in no way be described as an Oecumenical Council. If female episcopacy is invalid then so are any ordinations performed by that female bishop and thus the ramifications of B-005 affected the whole of the Episcopal Church. With the same process happening in the General Synod of the Church of England in 1992 where the ordination of women was passed by a narrow margin,[350] it was clear that any attempt to fulfil the vision glorious of Dr Pusey and the Oxford Movement was impossible. Thus, in America, the Continuing Anglican movement was born with a new jurisdiction and its mission and end is to become the very Church that the Tractarians envisage.

On answering the question, "What is an Anglican?" before he became the Anglican Catholic Archbishop, the then Fr Mark Haverland said:

> So how are we to define Anglicanism in this situation? It seems to me that there are two live possibilities before us. One possibility is that we define Anglicanism precisely by reference to its multiplicity of traditions and lack of uniformity, by its "comprehensiveness". This definition, however, reduces Anglicanism to liberal Protestantism and to the current state of collapse. The irony of Anglicanism-as-comprehensiveness

---

[348] For details of these clergymen, see Project Canterbury biographies, http://anglicanhistory.org/bios/ (Accessed 25th March 2021)
[349] Such as the Protestant Truth Society, set up by Kensit in 1889 but still extant.
[350] All three houses of the church body approved the measure by the necessary two-thirds majority vote, with bishops endorsing it 39-13, clergy 176-74 and laity 169-82.

is that persons with theological integrity have no desire to be comprehended by such a communion.

The other possible definition is in fact something of a redefinition: we may redefine Anglicanism by reference to one of its classical strands or parties and then assert that that single tradition should henceforth be normative to the exclusion of the other classical Anglican parties. If we take the first option, as the old Anglican Communion has done, we are doomed. The ACC, therefore, has adopted the second approach.[351]

The "classical strand" here is that of Anglo-Catholicism which grounds the identity of the ACC. It means that "Anglican" ceases to be a noun upon which the Formularies are pressed and Protestantism enshrined, but rather it becomes an adjective filled with history, heritage and commitment to the Faith once delivered to the saints. Just as he identifies Anglicanism as Protestant, H. A. Hodges sees Anglicanism as being in a unique position to be the Western Orthodox Church:

True Western Orthodoxy is to be found by bodies of western people, members of western nations coming with all their western background, their western habits and traditions into the circle of the Orthodox Faith. Then we should have an Orthodoxy which was really western because its memory was western – a memory of the Christian History of the West, not as the West now remembers it, but purged and set in perspective by the Orthodox Faith.[352]

This is something that the ACC, freed from the Erastian and Social influences of the Anglican Communion, can address together with its communion partners.

Conclusion

Is the ACC truly Anglican? First, it has been demonstrated that the ACC has preserved the Apostolic Succession of bishops in two strands, one through the Old Catholic Church and the Polish National Catholic Church through Bishops Pagtakhan and Chambers and also through the Episcopal Church through Bishop Chambers and with subsequent consecrations through bishops such as Bishop Br John-Charles Vockler who spent some time as an assistant bishop in dioceses in the Church of England. The fact that the first Continuing Anglican bishop, Bishop Doren was consecrated by two bishops, Chambers and Pagtakhan, albeit with consent from

---

[351] Archbishop Mark Haverland (then Fr), The Trinitarian, October 1995
[352] (Hodges, 1947) p 52

the two other intended consecrators, does not invalidate the succession especially since the express intent was to consecrate with four. Thus the ACC possesses Anglican and Catholic Orders.

Second, the ACC has a shared heritage with the Episcopal Church and Church of England, departing from each of these institutions in 1978 and 1992 respectively in the light of changes made to the Catholic Faith at the relevant Convention and Synod. Again, the intention of the Continuing Movement was to maximize the opportunities for intercommunion until provinces of the Anglican Communion fell away.

Third, the Book of Common Prayer is central to worship, setting the standards for all liturgy used by the ACC. The Book is to be read through the doctrine of the Primitive Church which colours how the various prayers and liturgy is intended.

The major departure from Anglicanism is the subordination of the Anglican Formularies to the Primitive Church, especially the adoption of the Seventh Oecumenical Council. The Books of Homilies which form part of the Formularies reference the first six but repudiate the seventh Council. This subordination is made clear by the very name of the Church. It is Catholic first and this is qualified by its Anglican heritage.

While the Protestant nature of Anglicanism is not always conducive to the preservation of the Catholic Faith, it is recognised that removing the purely Papal influences from the doctrine of the Church is intended to follow the Primitive Church but has been prevented from doing so by politics and the strong influence of Protestants within the Church. The Oxford Movement sought to regain the theology of the first fifteen hundred years of the Church of England but was prevented from doing so fully even despite some marked success in the century following the Assize Sermon of 1833. The separation of the ACC and its communion partners from the Anglican Communion has freed it to continue and complete the work of Pusey and Newman without the necessity of converting to the Roman Catholic Church but rather preserving the Anglican aspect of Catholicism which continued as a single thread through the history of the Church from the Reformation.

It is therefore quite reasonable that the claims to the Anglican nature of the ACC are well-founded and that it is truly a continuation of the Anglican Church which lost its way due to capitulation of Catholic doctrine to modern social influences rather than the Catholic Principles which brought her into being.

Conclusions and Further Directions

The Anglican Catholic Church is well-named. It is Catholic in its Ignatian sense in possessing bishops in the Apostolic Succession who administer to those who gather round the sacraments including the Body and Blood of Christ in the elements of the Eucharist. It is Catholic in its Cyrillic-Vincentian sense in that it holds to the faith of the Primitive Church and seeks to preserve that faith as fully as possible. It is Anglican in the sense that the richness of the expression of the Catholic Faith as received by the Church of England is preserved through its Apostolic Succession, History and Liturgy. It continues Anglicanism by retaining the mind of the Tractarians freed from obstructing influences.

It must be said, however, that the ACC as an institution in its own right is not yet forty-five years old – a mere moment in the eyes of a Church that has lasted a millennium or two. Its full identity as part of the Catholic Church is yet to be fully expressed and this can only come with time, study and prayer. The schisms and separations that occurred in the Continuing Movement at its origin and in the 1990s are beginning to heal. This makes it all the more important for the ACC to understand its identity in order to engage with the other branches of the Catholic Church of which it claims to be just a part. This means that there are several areas in which further study may prove beneficial.

The Principle of Theologoumena

Even though it describes itself as a continuation of the Primitive Church, it is clear that, even within that time there are issues that were not settled by the Oecumenical Councils. The example of the *filioque* has already been raised and it continues to divide the Eastern Church from the Western. In 1898 Vassily V. Bolotov and Aleksander L. Katanski put forward the idea of *theologoumena* with respect to the *filioque* in order to bring together Anglicans, Old Catholics and Eastern Orthodox Churches.

> "The *theologoumena* are the theological opinions of the holy Fathers of the one undivided Church: they are the opinions of those among whom are found persons we rightly call οἱ διδάσκασκαλοι τῆς οἰκουμένης. The dogma contains the

> *necessaria*, the *theologoumenon* the *dubia*: *In necessariis unitas. in dubiis libertas!*"[353]

Bolotov is quoting indirectly the Roman Catholic Archbishop Marco Antonio de Dominis of Split who says "*unitatem in necessariis, in non necessariis libertatem, in omnibus caritatem*"[354] This is the thinking that formed the underlay of the Elizabethan Settlement and even this failed to satisfy either the "Church Papists" or the Puritans but it managed to hold the High Church, the Lutherans and the Calvinists in some balance.

Yet, there is a further problem with the Settlement. Given the intention of the Book of Common Prayer to be patient of an interpretation of Catholic Principles then the Catholic Principles require that it **must** be interpreted according to the Catholic Principles which will rule out Receptionism in favour of the Real Presence. This is similar to the argument that given that God must exist in one possible world then He must exist in all possible worlds. Thus the ACC is mandated to a reading of its liturgy and worship which is in line with Catholic Doctrine. This poses problems especially in areas of doctrine which are not clear.

This is most obviously true in the varied beliefs within the ACC regarding Soteriology in which there are a range of views from Universalism to strict Augustinianism. One reason for this disparity lies within the Calvinist interpretation of the Articles which is still inherent in the older Anglican Catholics and the reaction against it by others. Others are finding the Orthodox Soteriology more convincing as the relationship with the Primitive Church is explored: this view is also countered by the Anglican Papalists who have remained apart from Rome seeing the Ordinariate as insufficient for preserving an Anglican culture. Thus there is still need within the ACC for a form of the Elizabethan Settlement to allow for legitimate differences of opinion until a greater understanding and consensus is discerned within the Church. The Affirmation states:

> The conscience, as the inherent knowledge of right and wrong, cannot stand alone as a sovereign arbiter of morals. Every Christian is obligated to form his conscience by the Divine

---

[353] Quoted in Ioannis Zizioulas, Uniformity, diversity and the unity of the Church, *Internationale kirchliche Zeitschrift : neue Folge der Revue internationale de théologie* 91 (2001) p 53

[354] Marco Antonio de Dominis, (1617), De republica ecclesiastica libri X, VI. Viii Archbishop de Dominis, himself, quarrelled with the Pope and fled to England where he was involved in the consecrations of two bishops in 1617, thereby entwining Roman Catholic Succession with Anglican.

Moral Law and the Mind of Christ as revealed in Holy Scriptures, and by the teaching and Tradition of the Church.

Its first point following this is that, "[a]ll people, individually and collectively, are responsible to their Creator for their acts, motives, thoughts and words, since 'we must all appear before the judgment seat of Christ…'" How the ACC approaches its soteriology is another matter, but there is a clear commitment to *theologoumena* which allows for relationships with other Continuing Anglican bodies such as the United Episcopal Church.

Modernism

The principle of *theologoumena* can only go so far, however. The Continuing Anglican movement started precisely because changes were made to the nature of the sacraments that cannot be supported by Holy Scripture or Tradition. The Vincentian Canon does not support the ordination of women to the Sacred Priesthood, nor can this issue be put to an Oecumenical Council until the Church is capable once more of meeting in such a way. Even then, the fact remains that if God had given the Church authority to ordain women, this would have been recognizable from the start and thus, it appears highly unlikely that this will ever be part of Catholic Doctrine.

The idea of the Church being "modernised" is something that has been fought since the sixteenth century; indeed, the English Reformers sincerely believed that they were trying to redress innovations brought in during the tenth and eleventh centuries by returning to the Primitive Church. Modernism relies on the idea that the understanding and learning of the present age are necessarily superior to the deposit of faith accrued over the centuries according to the Catholic Principles. Indeed, it may be seen in such modern approaches as the Jesus Seminar that materialistic and Humean presuppositions have been used to conclude that the Historical Jesus is a moral teacher who did not believe that He was the Son of God.

The ACC has adapted itself to the current milieu, embracing modern technology and social media into which it has become one voice among a cacophony of others. The COVID 19 Pandemic has changed how people worship and thus further study is needed into the impact of the pandemic on evangelism and how the ACC continues its unchanging faith in the changing world.

Further, the growing antipathy of the secular culture to traditional Christian morality is of concern and one direction that is perhaps worth exploring is the Anglican Catholic justification of why the ancient understanding of Christian morality has a firmer philosophical and theological base and is genuinely more loving than the present understanding which threatens to distract Christians from the practice of holiness and their participation in the covenant with Almighty God.

Unity

The ACC has trademarked its name but it cannot trademark the term "Anglican Catholic". This might be seen as problematic in that there exist Christians calling themselves Anglican Catholic who do not hold to the Catholic Faith as understood by Continuing Anglicans and who mean something quite different by the term. While this is unfortunate, it sets up an excellent opportunity for the current movement towards organic unity among Continuing Anglicans. In not owning the term "Anglican Catholic", and in seeing itself as one *part* of the Catholic Church, it allows others who hold the same heritage and theological outlook to be embraced by the term "Anglican Catholic". Thus, the current concordat between the ACC, the Anglican Church in America, the Anglican Province of America and the Diocese of the Holy Cross is indeed a concordat between Anglican Catholics in the larger sense detailed here in this essay. Whatever the name of the hoped-for organic union may be, it will nonetheless bear witness to the Anglican Catholicism of its members.

Struggle

The ACC has had to fight for its existence. In places such as the United Kingdom, it has been a fight to survive the many comings and goings of strong personalities with their own agendas. There has been a fight to gain access to buildings in which to offer the prayers, praises and sacrifices which make up the Catholic Church's duty. There is an ongoing fight to proclaim the Gospel against the noise of the world and the many different perturbations and deviations which are being sounded therefrom. This is how it should be, for the Lord says:

> if any man will come after me, let him deny himself, and take up his cross, and follow me.[355]

Struggle, pain, suffering and hardship are facts of life: they are the consequences of billions of disordered wills bumbling about throughout the immensity of time on this little planet called Earth. This is a direct result of the disobedience of our first parents as God says to Adam:

> Because thou hast hearkened unto the voice of thy wife, and hast eaten of the tree, of which I commanded thee , saying , Thou shalt not eat of it: cursed is the ground for thy sake; in sorrow shalt thou eat of it all the days of thy life; Thorns also

---

[355] St Matthew xvi.24

> and thistles shall it bring forth to thee; and thou shalt eat the herb of the field; In the sweat of thy face shalt thou eat bread, till thou return unto the ground; for out of it wast thou taken : for dust thou art, and unto dust shalt thou return.[356]

As the Israelites enter the wilderness from the luxury-become-slavery of Egypt, so Continuing Anglicans have left the material comforts of a wealthy institution in order to continue and pursue the Catholic Faith. They rely on one hard but simple fact: suffering is inevitable and God is faithful. To be an Anglican Catholic is to turn this struggle into a glorious combat against the rule of individual passions by adhering closely to the Faith once delivered to the saints. It is a challenge that requires bravery, integrity, a passion for self-improvement within the context of the Church, and Kipling's[357] indifference to success and disappointment. It is the noble challenge, no matter what, to gather communities around the Church's bishops and thus embody Christ's love for the fallen world. Like the Orthodox, the Anglican Catholic must not only carry his cross but also venerate it and thus, in union with Christ, make his suffering a sacrifice whereby the business of being human is sanctified. If this were easy, it would not be worth doing. If this were easy then humanity would be a pale shadow of what it really is.

For Anglican Catholics, the fight for the Christian Faith goes on and will continue until Christ comes again in glory. *Maranatha.*

Final words

The ACC is not a well-known institution and is still exploring the ramifications of its institutional beginnings in the Congress of St Louis. What is clear is that it has a firm institutional base and *raison d'être* upon which to build and grow. Whatever challenges it faces, the ACC falls back upon the integrity of its holding of the Catholic Faith which it shares with so many other Christians, praying for the salvation of all and preaching the love of God and neighbour in obedience to the commandments of Our Lord to whom be all worship, praise, honour, power and glory with God the Father in the unity of the Holy Ghost, ever One God, world without end.

---

[356] Genesis iii.17-19
[357] Rudyard Kipling, "If…"

REFERENCES

Akin, Jimmy. 2010. *The Fathers know best.* San Diego : Catholic Answers, 2010.

Anglican Catholic Church. *Canons.*

Bede. 1999. *The Ecclesiastical History of the English People.* Oxford : OUP, 1999.

Benedict XVI, Pope. 2007. *The Apostles.* New York : Our Sunday Visitor, 2007.

Bess, Douglas. 2006. *Divided We Stand: A History of the Continuing Anglican Movement.* Berkeley, CA : Apocryphile Press, 2006.

Bettensen, Henry and Maunder, Chris. 1999. *Documents of the Christian Church.* Oxford : OUP, 1999.

Bicknell, E. J. and Carpenter, Rev H. J. 1939. *A Theological Introduction to the Thirty Nine Articles.* London : Longmans, Green and Co, 1939.

Bray, Gerald. 1994. *Documents of the English Reformation.* Cambridge : James Clarke and Co Ltd, 1994.

Browne, E. H. 1887. *An Exposition of the Thirty-Nine Articles.* London : Longmans, Green & Co, 1887.

Chandler, Michael. 2003. *An Introduction to the Oxford Movement.* London : SPCK, 2003.

Chapman, Mark. 2012. *Anglican Theology.* London : T & T Clark, 2012.

Chapman, Mark, Clarke, Sathianathan and Percy, Martin. 2015. *The Oxford Handbook of Anglican Studies.* Oxford : OUP, 2015.

Clarke, W. K. Lowther and Harris, Charles. 1964. *Liturgy and Worship.* London : SPCK, 1964.

Craig, William L. 2010. *On Guard.* Ontario, Canada : David Cook, 2010.

—. **2008.** *Reasonable Faith.* Wheaton, Illinois : Crossway, 2008.

Craig, William Lane and Moreland, J. P. 2003. *Philosophical Foundations for a Christian Worldview.* Downers Grove, IL : InterVarsity Press, 2003.

Damick, Fr Andrew Stephen. 2011. *Orthodoxy and Heterodoxy.* Chesterton IN : Ancient Faith Publishing, 2011.

Dawkins, Richard. 2006. *The God Delusion.* London : Bantam, 2006.

Denzinger, Heinrich. 2012. *Compendium of Creeds, Definitions, and Declarations on Matters of Faith and Morals (43rd Edition) .* San Fransisco : Ignatius, 2012.

Donaldson, James and Roberts, Alexander. 1994 (Reprinted 2012). *The Church Fathers - Ante-Nicene Fathers.* Peabody, Massachusetts : Henderson Publishers Marketing, 1994 (Reprinted 2012).

Ehrman, Bart. 2012. *Did Jesus Exist?* New York : HarperOne, 2012.

—. **2015.** *How Jesus became God.* s.l. : Bravo Ltd, 2015.

—. **2009.** *Jesus Interrupted: Revealing the hidden contradictions in the Bible.* New York, NY : HarperOne, 2009.

Englezakis, Benedict. 1982. *New And Old in God's Revelation.* Cambridge : James Clarke and Co, 1982.

Evans, Craig A. 2007. *Fabricating Jesus: How Modern Scholars Distort the Gospels.* Nottingham, UK : IVP, 2007.

Feser, Edward. 2008. *The Last Superstition: A refutation of the New Atheism.* South Bend, Indiana : St Augustine's Press, 2008.

Guarino, Thomas G. 2013. *Vincent of Lerins and the Development of Christian Doctrine.* Grand Rapids, MI : Baker Academic, 2013.

Haigh, Christopher. 1993. *English Reformations.* Oxford : OUP, 1993.

Haverland, Most Rev Dr Mark. 3rd Ed 2011. *Anglican Catholic Faith and Practice.* s.l. : Anglican Parishes Association, 3rd Ed 2011.

Hodges, H. A. 1947. *Anglicanism and Orthodoxy.* London : SCM Press, 1947.

Holmes, Michael W. 2007. *The Apostolic Fathers: Greek Texts and English Translations, 3rd Edition.* Grand Rapids,MI : Baker Academic, 2007.

Johnson, Luke Timothy. 1997. *The Real Jesus.* New York, NY : HarperOne, 1997.

Jurgens, William A. 1970. *The Faith of the Early Fathers (3 volumes).* Collegeville Minnesota : The Liturgical Press, 1970.

Kirk, Geoffrey. 2016. *Without Precedent.* Eugene, OR : Wipf and Stock, 2016.

Komoszewski, J. Ed, Sawyer, M. James and Wallace, Daniel. 2006. *Reinventing Jesus.* Grand Rapids, MI : Kregel, 2006.

Landon, Fr Edward H. 1942?. *A Manual of Councils of the Holy Catholic Church.* London : Griffith Farran and Co, 1942?

McCann, Abbot Justin (transl). 1952. *Rule of St Benedict.* London : Burns and Oates, 1952.

McGrath, Alister E. 2001. *Christian Theology: An Introduction.* Malden, MA : Blackwell, 2001.

Middleton, Arthur. 2001. *Fathers and Anglicans: the Limits of Orthodoxy.* Bodmin : Gracewing, 2001.

More, Paul E. and Cross, Frank L. 1935. *Anglicanism.* London : SPCK, 1935.

Moreland, J.P. and Craig, William Lane. 2003. *Philosophical Foundations for a Christian Worldview.* Downers Grove, IL : IVP, 2003.

Moss, Fr Claude Beaufort. 1965. *The Christian Faith.* London : SPCK, 1965.

—. **1957.** *The Church of England and the Seventh Council.* London : Faith Press, 1957.

Munn, Fr Jonathan. 2019. *Anglican Catholicism: Unchanging Faith in a Changing World.* Lydd : Lulu.com, 2019.

—. **2019.** *Mindful of Man: Part 1 God, Man and Love.* Lydd : Lulu.com, 2019.

Need, Stephen W. 2008. *Truly Divine and Truly Human.* London : SPCK, 2008.

New, John F. H. 1964. *Anglican and Puritan: The Basis of Their Opposition, 1558-1640.* Stanford, California : Stanford University Press, 1964.

Newman, St John Henry. 1993. *Apologia Pro Vita Sua.* London : Everyman, 1993.

Nichols O.P, Aidan. 1994. *The Panther and the Hind.* Edinburgh : T & T Clark, 1994.

Ott, Dr Ludwig. 1952. *Fundamentals of Catholic Dogma.* Rockford, Illinois : TAN, 1952.

Pickering, W. S. F. 1989. *Anglo-Catholicism: A Study in Religious Ambiguity.* Cambridge : James Clarke & Co, 1989.

Quasten, Johannes. 2000. *Patrology (In four volumes).* Notre Dame, IN : Ave Maria Press, 2000.

Ratzinger, Cardinal Joseph. 2003. *God Is Near Us: The Eucharist, The Heart of Life.* s.l. : Ignatius Press, 2003.

Rowell, Geoffrey. 1983. *The Vision Glorious.* Oxford : Clarendon Press, 1983.

Schaff, Dr Philip (ed). 2004. *Nicene and Post-Nicene Fathers (1st Series).* Peabody, Massachusetts : Hendrickson Publishers Inc, 2004.

Schaff, Dr Philip and Wace, Dr Henry (eds). 1996. *The Nicene and Post-Nicene Fathers (2nd Series).* Edinburgh : T&T Clark, 1996.

Sedgwick, Peter H. 2019. *The Origins of Anglican Moral Theology.* Boston, MA : Brill, 2019.

Siecienski, A Edward. 2012. *The Filioque: History Of A Doctrinal Controversy* . s.l. : OUP, 2012.

Sykes, Stephen, Booty, John and Knight, Jonathan. 1988. *The Study of Anglicanism.* Minneapolis, Minnesota : SPCK, 1988.

Tavard, George H. 1963. *The Quest for Catholicity.* London : The Catholic Book Club, 1963.

Various. 1979. *The Philokalia (in four volumes) compiled by St Nikodemos of the Holy Mountain and St Makarios of Corinth.* s.l. : Faber and Faber, 1979.

Vatican. 2002. *Catechism of the Catholic Church.* Vatican City : Continuum, 2002.

Wallace (ed), Daniel B. 2011. *Revisiting the Corruption of the New Testament.* Great Rapids : Kregel, 2011.

Walsham, Alexandra. 1993. *Church Papists.* Woodbridge : The Boydell Press, 1993.

Ward, Keith. 2009. *The God Conclusion.* London : Darton, Longman and Todd Ltd, 2009.

Williams, Peter J. 2018. *Can we trust the Gospels?* Wheaton, Illinois : Crossway, 2018.

Wobbermin, G. 1899. *Bishop Serapion's Prayer book.* London : SPCK, 1899.

Wright, Tom. 1992. *Who was Jesus?* London : SPCK, 1992.